The Complete Guide to

PATIOS & WALKWAYS

Moneysaving Do-it-yourself Projects for Improving Outdoor Living Space

Creative Publishing
international

MINNEAPOLIS, MINNESOTA
www.creativepub.com

Creative Publishing international

Copyright © 2010
Creative Publishing international, Inc.
400 First Avenue North, Suite 300
Minneapolis, Minnesota 55401
1-800-328-0590
www.creativepub.com
All rights reserved

Printed in China

10 9 8 7 6 5 4 3

Library of Congress Cataloging-in-Publication Data

The complete guide to patios & walkways : money-saving
do-it-yourself projects for improving outdoor living space.
        p. cm.
    Includes index.
    At heaf of title: Black and Decker.
    Summary: "A comprehensive guide to plan, build, maintain, repair,
and accessorize great outdoor living spaces"--Provided
by publisher.
    ISBN-13: 978-1-58923-481-9 (soft cover)
    ISBN-10: 1-58923-481-2 (soft cover)
    1. Patios--Amateurs' manuals. 2. Garden walks--Amateurs'
manuals. I. Black & Decker Corporation (Towson, Md.) II. Title.

TH4970.C647 2010
690'.893--dc22

2009038316

The Complete Guide to Patios & Walkways
Created by: The Editors of Creative Publishing international, Inc. in cooperation with Black & Decker. Black & Decker® is a trademark of The
Black & Decker Corporation and is used under license.

President/CEO: Ken Fund

Home Improvement Group

Publisher: Bryan Trandem
Managing Editor: Tracy Stanley
Senior Editor: Mark Johanson
Editor: Jennifer Gehlhar

Creative Director: Michele Lanci-Altomare
Art Direction/Design: Jon Simpson, Brad Springer, James Kegley

Lead Photographer: Joel Schnell
Set Builder: James Parmeter
Production Managers: Linda Halls, Laura Hokkanen

Page Layout Artists: Hespenheide Design
Shop Help: Charles Boldt
Author: Philip Schmidt
Copy Editor: Betsey Matheson
Proofreader: Jane Hilken
Illustrator: Trevor Burks

Cover Photo by Beth Singer © 2009

Contents

The Complete Guide to
Patios & Walkways

57

116

64

120

70

132

84

144

89

150

96

206

106

236

Introduction

A well-appointed patio is the perfect example of enhanced outdoor living space. Designed around your lifestyle and favorite leisure activities, a patio can be comfortable, spacious, and even versatile, just like any well-used indoor gathering place. But what makes a patio so special are the things you can't get under your roof: pure sunlight, open air, an atmosphere that changes hourly and with the seasons—in short, a direct connection to the outdoors. It is this unique combination of comfort and the natural world that gives patios the power to lure us out of the house and away from our indoor routines.

As an "outdoor room," designing and decorating a new patio is not so different from planning any other living space. The design rule "function comes first" certainly applies. Assessing how everyone in the household will use the new patio is the primary consideration that influences every other decision, from planning the size, shape, and layout to choosing paving materials and adding special features and amenities.

One of the great things about building a new patio or walkway is the number of options you have to choose from. Few other building projects offer so many choices of materials, configurations, and even locations—unlike a deck or balcony, a patio doesn't have to be tied to the house or confined to the back yard; it can welcome guests at the front door or host an intimate gathering around a fire pit in a far corner of your lot. With all of this flexibility, a patio can complement your home's architecture as much as it shapes your landscape, and that's what makes creating a patio from scratch such a rewarding project.

If a patio is a stage from which you can enjoy the outdoors, walkways and paths are the ties that bring it all together, linking the house, patio, garden, lawn, driveway, and any other points in between. Pathways unify various landscape elements in both functional and perceptual ways: they define spaces, direct traffic, and make it easy to travel from one place to the next. They also draw a line between separate, sometimes distant, spaces—joining them visually and inviting us to venture on to the next destination. Thinking about patios and walkways together is a smart choice, as both can transform an outdoor home. It's not surprising, then, that a new patio project often leads to new walkways as well.

Whether you're dreaming of a new patio, a new walkway, or both, this book will take you through the process from start to finish—from gathering ideas and choosing materials to preparing the site and laying the surface. After surfacing, you can set out some furniture and enjoy the fruits of your labor or you can gather more tools and start right in on another project, such as installing landscape lights or building an outdoor kitchen. Either way, as soon as you begin to enjoy your new patio, you'll quickly understand why so many do-it-yourselfers see their patios as works in progress—it's fun to keep thinking up new and creative ways to make your favorite outdoor spaces even better.

Patio & Walkway Basics

To install a new patio or walkway, first get started by working through the basic steps of planning your project. The section in this chapter on design themes can help you think conceptually about the character and emotional quality of your new outdoor room. Consider, also, all of the ways you hope to use the new space and decide how the layout and other design elements will best accommodate those activities.

Next comes the choice of paving material. Whether it's classic clay brick, naturally rough-hewn flagstone, simple and sleek concrete, or any of the other great options you'll learn about here, the surface material you choose will be the defining feature of your patio or path.

In addition to the appearance and performance qualities of the different paving options, make sure to think about the logistics of installation. Flip ahead to the step-by-step projects in this book and review the materials to get an idea of the work involved and to gauge which applications best suit your design, budget, and time frame. Other practical matters to consider—including zoning restrictions and natural conditions on your property, such as drainage and seasonal weather—are addressed in this chapter as well.

When it's time to pull it all together, you'll find it helpful to draft a site plan. The patio and walkway plans on pages 33 to 37 offer inspiration and tips for thinking globally about your patio or walkway in the context of your outdoor home.

In this chapter:
- Design Themes for Patios
- Material Selection
- Practical Considerations
- Patio & Walkway Plans

Design Themes for Patios

If you were planning new living spaces for your indoor home, you would probably start by listing the main uses of each room—cooking meals, throwing parties, relaxing with the family, sitting down for a chat with the neighbors, etc. Keeping these desired uses in mind, you then decide how each space should look and feel. What is the essential character, or theme, of the space? Should it be formal and intimate, or should it have an open feel, with casual furnishings setting the tone for each activity? The same thought process applies to designing a new patio (which is, in essence, an outdoor living space). The following discussion of patio design themes can help get you started.

Entertaining & Dining

If a patio is perfect for one thing, it's alfresco meals. Whether enjoying a meal with the family or throwing a casual weekend barbeque or late-night hors d'oeuvre party, food just tastes better outdoors. A patio intended for everyday meals should be casual and convenient. Having a table and chairs set up at all times lets you decide at the last minute to eat outside without much fuss. Choose lighting that is bright enough for eating comfortably but can easily be lowered for after-dinner conversation. Locating the patio just off your indoor kitchen makes the space convenient enough to be used as a second dining room. On the other hand, an outdoor kitchen brings the cooking right into the space, so the cook is never stuck inside during those precious summer evenings.

Entertaining on a patio involves a special combination of indoor comforts and outdoor pleasures, where the open atmosphere invites guests to lounge under the stars or take a stroll through the garden. A well-designed entertainment space should be roomy yet comfortable. Overheads and walls promote a feeling of intimacy, while a wide walkway or broad steps can encourage guests to wander off the patio and into the yard. Furniture and more permanent features, such as a fireplace, bar, or large dining table, can define the room's layout and set the stage for specific activities. Lighting is critical for setting the mood and should be adjustable for tailoring your patio space to different settings.

A simple dining setup with easy access to the kitchen is ideal for everything from morning coffee to romantic dinners to late-afternoon cocktails.

Aside from the obvious focal point created by an outdoor fireplace or other similar large structure, an open patio can be entirely defined by its furniture and can be completely rearranged to suit the occasion.

The shelter of plants and overheads can be an especially welcome feature for dining and entertaining areas, blocking the glare and heat of direct sunlight.

Private

When you want to be outside, but don't want to feel exposed or on display, a private patio space is the answer. Privacy can take many forms and often is as much a result of perception as physical seclusion. Adding privacy might mean screening out the views of neighbors or locating the patio in a distant corner of the lot. A fountain or other water feature can provide a sense of privacy by drowning out noise and letting you dwell in your own thoughts. Along with increased privacy comes a feeling of enclosure and shelter, which may result in a space that is intimate but may be somewhat limited functionally. If this is not what you want for your entire patio, you can always make some parts private while leaving others open. Another option is to build a small private retreat away from the main patio. Whatever the design, a private patio should be personal and comfortable, particularly for those who will spend the most time there.

Urban patios often rely on tall fences or walls for much needed privacy. Plantings help soften the look of the barriers and prevent a closed-in feeling.

Expansive

This sprawling outdoor room maintains an expansive feel with a visual flow between levels. Accents of boulders and trees that echo the view of distant mountains blend this patio into the natural openness of the land.

The most important idea behind expansive patios is openness. Where private spaces are sanctuaries closed off from the outer world, an expansive patio unfolds into the broader landscape, often blending with its surroundings.

Wide open patio designs are typically favored on lots that are large enough not to need privacy and in yards that offer a great view. However, creating an expansive feel is not about maximizing the patio's size. In fact, small patios can gain the most from an expansive theme—leaving patios open allows them to borrow views of the natural landscape and create the perception of increased space.

This basic concept of openness also informs the layout and decoration of expansive patios. Designs are most often very simple, with no walls or large plantings that would block views or muddle the balance of the overall lot plan. Unobtrusive pots or shrubs placed to the side can help frame the view from the patio, but a large overhead might be too oppressive and can detract from the open feeling. An expansive theme works well for remote outdoor rooms as well as patios right next to the house.

Remote

Most patios are located right behind the house, but there's no rule saying they have to be. A freestanding or detached patio can be remote both literally and psychologically. A remote space can be private, tucked behind dense foliage at the end of a path, or it can be open and expansive in feel—a comfortable perch for taking in a view or catching the sunset.

Making your outdoor room out of the way inspires creativity—being free of the style constraints set by the house, the patio can blend into the landscape or become an eye-catching focal point on its own. Detached patios are often created to supplement a patio or deck adjoining the house. This arrangement offers even more freedom for designing the remote patio, since the primary outdoor activities can take place on the main patio close to the house, while the remote space is used ostensibly as a private retreat.

A remote patio is ideal for a private retreat. Being away from the house, it can take on a unique architecture to elicit a particular mood. Here, a classical romantic setting allows the homeowners to feel as though they are far away when they are just in the back corner of the yard.

Multipurpose

Indoors, people congregate in their multifunctional spaces—namely the kitchen and family room. The same is true for patios: when the outdoor layout and features cater to multiple activities, the space tends to be used more often. After all, the purpose of a patio is to help you enjoy your home's outdoor space.

While a multipurpose patio requires careful planning, it doesn't have to be all about practicality. Centering the layout around a functional dining area, for example, doesn't mean you can't include a natural garden plot, a decorative water feature, or a sequestered nook for a private reading space. The ideal plan is dynamic enough to accommodate your household's range of activities, yet remains unified in design and appearance. A broad view of the patio (which is most often the view from the house) should reveal an integrated layout with a natural flow from one area to another.

This multipurpose patio includes a built-in firepit on one side and a cozy spot for a bistro set on the other. The open area in the middle provides access to a screened gazebo for all-season recreation.

Welcoming

Not all patios need to be hidden behind the house. Often surrounding the front door or main entrance, welcoming patios are a warm greeting to visitors and can be an attractive link between the house and a driveway or public sidewalk.

The inviting appearance of an entry patio certainly adds curb appeal, but its true purpose is the same as any standard back yard space. In terms of use,

the entry patio is a return to the concept of the traditional front porch: a semiprivate space that allows homeowners to enjoy the outdoors while keeping in touch with neighbors. Being in full view, however, does place certain stylistic and architectural constraints on an entry patio. As the foreground to a home's façade, it's important that the patio complements the home's proportions and decorative scheme.

A charming walkway and casual sitting area convey a message of welcome and leisure to visitors of this house, as well as providing the perfect spot for spending warm evenings. The low gate adds a sense of privacy and closure to the patio area.

Sheltering

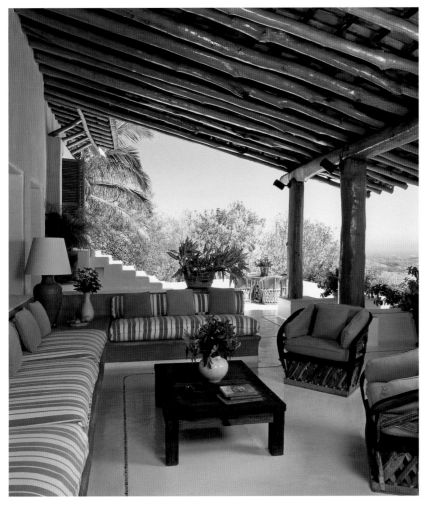

This timber-frame awning shades the patio below and plays a significant architectural role as the ceiling of the outdoor room.

A patio shelter can be anything from a garden trellis covered in flowering vines to a permanent, built-in overhead that makes the patio livable in all kinds of weather. Arbors and pergolas are the most popular types of patio overheads, and both are simple structures that lend themselves easily to personal creative touches.

Arbors are at home almost anywhere in the landscape, from front entryways to secluded gardens. On a patio, an arbor can serve as a dramatic entrance portal, a framework for climbing plants, or a cozy shelter for a corner seating area. The basic design of a wooden arbor includes two or four posts with a simple slatted roof. The sides between the posts can be left open or covered with trelliswork for supporting plants or adding privacy.

Pergolas are a step up from arbors in size and stature but are based on similar post-and-beam construction. In its traditional form, a pergola extends from the side or roof of a building to create a semi-shaded area linking the building with the outdoor landscape. Pergolas work equally well as freestanding structures, with four or more columns supporting large roof beams topped with a series of cross beams or slats. Add a pergola to create an attractive ceiling—or the suggestion of a ceiling—over a large section of your patio. Cover your pergola along the top with vines or fabric to gain privacy beneath the view of neighbors' upper-floor windows.

Careful placement of the overhead slats on patio shelters lets you enjoy sun or shade at specific times of the day. For example, if the summer sun is too hot at midday, angle the slats toward the morning sun while blocking out the hottest rays at midday and into the afternoon. But remember, any shading on an attached patio may limit the amount of natural light that reaches the house.

Material Selection

Brick, stone, and concrete rightly make up most people's short list of good patio and walkway surfaces, but these materials in their basic forms are just the beginning. Brick alone comes in a range of colors, textures, and styles, while the availability of stone and the variety of concrete pavers are both constantly expanding. After giving some thought to your preferred flooring surface, it will be well worth it to spend a few hours browsing local stone yards, landscape suppliers, and building centers to see what's available in your area. Ask about delivery pricing while you're there.

Brick

Natural clay brick is generally considered the most classic surface material for patios and walkways—a well-deserved distinction. With its combination of warm, natural coloring and texture and its orderly geometric shapes, brick is the perfect blend of house and garden. And with its small unit size, brick is also quite versatile and can be easily applied to formal layouts or imaginative curved patterns. The standard brick patio installation consists of setting brick into a sand bed in an ordered pattern, but brick can also be mortared over a concrete patio slab or walkway for a highly finished appearance and a surface that won't be affected by ground movement.

Bricks for outdoor floor surfaces are called pavers. These flat, solid units have a porous texture that helps provide traction in wet weather. Brick dimensions vary by manufacturer and range approximately from 1⅛ to 2¾" in thickness. The standard size (width and length) for sandset (mortarless) installation is 4 × 8". Bricks for mortared jobs are a little smaller to account for the mortar joints. Pavers are also rated for load-bearing strength and weather resistance. Types 2 and 3 are suitable for heavy foot traffic. SX (or SW) brick is for cold climates, MX brick is for warm climates without a hard frost, and NX brick is for interior applications. Don't use standard wall brick, fire brick, or other types of building brick for flooring surfaces.

Clay paving brick has a warm, classic feel that appeals to many homeowners. This traditional paving material is sure to add value to your home as well.

Concrete Pavers

Concrete pavers are the most popular alternative to traditional brick and are installed the same way—either sandset or mortared over a concrete slab. Like brick, concrete pavers are highly durable, and their uniform dimensions make them easy to work with. While most clay bricks only come in standard rectangular units, concrete pavers are available in a wide range of sizes and shapes, including small and large rectangles and squares, various interlocking designs, and trapezoidal shapes used for circular and fan patterns.

Concrete pavers can be manufactured with different textures and edge treatments that can greatly alter their appearance. Among the most popular styles are "tumbled" pavers that have softened, randomly chipped edges, giving the paving an age-worn look. The tumbled effect is an important component of the many cobblestone styles of concrete paving. For sandset installations, you can use virtually any type of concrete paver. Many come with spacing lugs molded into the sides of each unit—these automatically set an even space between pavers that you fill with sand to complete the installation (most clay bricks don't have spacing lugs, and you have to set the gaps with temporary spacers). For mortared finishes, choose concrete pavers with square sides (with or without spacing lugs); interlocking styles and other irregular shapes make it difficult to fill and finish the mortar joints.

Concrete paver products have evolved from commercial-looking units in basic pink and tan tones to a diverse assortment of colors, shapes, and textures. Pavers are now commonly available in sets of blended colors and shapes for a more natural look; they are tumbled with nicely variegated patterns.

Stone

Natural stone has an organic beauty that's unmatched by all other building materials. Stone paving is used all over the world in grand courtyards, ancient roadways, and back yard landscapes alike. In nature, stones frequently form paths for crossing streams and skirting muddy fields—it's not surprising, then, that it's a popular material for patios and walkways. Stone is available in many forms, while the most commonly used types for do-it-yourself projects are flagstone and stone tile.

Flagstone

Flagstone is the general term given to any broad, flat stone that has been split to a thickness of around one to four inches, making it good for paving. Common species of flagstone include sandstone, limestone, bluestone, and slate. Individual stones may have cut edges for paving in linear patterns, while stones with jagged edges and irregular shapes are best for creating a patio or walkway surface with a natural, casual feel.

Flagstones can be set in sand or stable (tamped) soil, or they can be permanently laid in mortar over a concrete patio slab or walkway. For an organic, stepping-stone effect, you can space stones widely and fill the gaps with gravel or groundcover plantings.

Availability of flagstone varies by region; see what types are offered at local stone yards. For paving on patios and primary walkways, make sure the stone is thick enough for furniture and/or heavy foot traffic and that the surface of the stones won't become dangerously slick when wet.

The beauty, strength, and unique character of stone makes it a natural choice for all sorts of hardscaping, especially patios, walkways, and garden paths. Paving a path with stones of varying shapes and sizes is just one way to create a one-of-a-kind paving surface.

Natural flagstone is cleft into slabs with irregular shapes and an often interesting, flaky top surface. Flagstone is also available in precut tiles.

Stone Tile

Many types of stone can be cut into flat, square, or rectangular tiles for outdoor paving. Slate, granite, marble, limestone, and quartzite are among the most common species of stone tile. In contrast to uncut flagstone's natural variation in thickness, shape, and texture, stone tile is more uniform and closer in appearance to manufactured tile. Its visual effect is a nice combination of natural texture and coloring with orderly geometric patterns.

Most stone tile is too thin to support foot traffic when laid over a soft base and must be installed in mortar over a concrete slab. For thicker tiles and stronger species of stone suitable for sandset paving, check with local suppliers. It's important to discuss your plans with your tile supplier, as not all tiles are suitable for all applications, especially outdoors. A local tile dealer will know what works best in your local climate.

Buying Stone ▸

Flagstone is typically sold by the square yard or by the ton. Before you start shopping, calculate the area of your patio in square feet. Stone suppliers can use this number to estimate your requirements in tons, if necessary. Buying flagstone in bulk from a stone yard is less expensive than hand-selecting individual stones, though you don't get to inspect all of the pieces in advance. Also, purchasing bulk shipments preloaded onto pallets helps prevent breakage before and during delivery. To estimate quantities of stone tile, calculate the total area you need to cover, then factor in the thickness of the grout joints. Your tile supplier can help with these calculations.

Here are some other things to think about when considering stone for your patio or walkway:

- In general, the difficulty of quarrying and dressing stone makes it a relatively expensive material. The more work that's done to the raw material—hand-selection, cutting, and finishing—the higher the cost.
- When it comes to a finished patio, one of the main drawbacks of some flagstone is its uneven surface, which can lead to wobbly tables and the occasional stubbed toe. However, many people choose stone specifically for its natural "imperfections."
- Softer flagstone, such as sandstone, can split fairly easily if not supported evenly from below. Sandstone is also vulnerable to scratches from shovels, chair legs, and other metal objects.
- Slate and some other types of flagstone and tile can be slippery when wet—an important consideration for exposed surfaces.

At the other end of the spectrum from irregular, cleft flagstone, stone tile surfaces are orderly and refined. Yet, even with precise, formal patterns like this, the natural coloring of stone adds an organic quality that you don't get with most manufactured tile.

Poured Concrete

Most new homes today that include outdoor patios or walkways utilize poured concrete surfaces. Concrete is the default outdoor surface for several reasons: it's the cheapest of the hardscape materials, it's extremely durable and virtually maintenance-free, and it involves the quickest installation (especially for a professional concrete crew). Also, if the homeowners don't like the look of bare concrete, it can always be covered with another outdoor material or stained to add a permanent touch of color.

The same benefits hold true for a do-it-yourselfer building a new concrete patio or walkway. While a big concrete pour is a challenging undertaking for amateurs, a walkway or even a small patio is certainly a doable project. The secret to success is taking the time to prepare the site properly, stake your forms well, and watch the wet concrete carefully as it sets up so you'll know when to begin the finishing steps.

For first-timers, it's always a good idea to start with something small, such as a walkway or small utility slab, to learn the overall process and the nuances of finishing concrete before you tackle a bigger project.

A poured concrete slab or walkway can be a finished surface by itself, or it can serve as the structural foundation for other surface materials, including mortared brick and concrete pavers, stone, and tile. In fact, mortared finishes must be laid over a stable concrete foundation—soil or even compacted gravel may cause the mortar to crack. Whether you're leaving the concrete bare or you're planning to cover it with a mortared-in material, the basic construction steps for building the slab are the same, though a bare concrete slab requires a little more finishing to ensure a smooth surface. Another popular use of poured concrete is building walkways with concrete molds, as shown on pages 156 to 159.

Smooth, flat, and reassuringly solid, a poured concrete surface is the best option for those who want a level flooring surface that sweeps clean and stays put virtually forever.

Decorative Effects for Poured Concrete

While many people like the clean, monolithic look of a plain concrete slab, there are several options for adding decorative touches to a new concrete surface:

Seeded concrete is finished with a layer of fine stones for a uniform, yet organic, effect. This is a popular choice for patios because of its multicolored, textured appearance and nonslip surface.

A divided concrete slab is poured with permanent wood dividers and border edging, separating the slab into equal sections. In addition to its decorative value, a divided slab is also easier to work with, since it allows you to pour and finish one section at a time, if desired.

Tinting and acid staining introduce a range of color options to the familiar cement gray of plain concrete. Commercial colorants, available in both liquid and powdered forms, can be added to wet concrete mix for consistent color throughout the material. This is a good option for mold-formed walkways and other projects that call for small batches of wet concrete. For larger projects, you can order ready-mix concrete in a limited range of colors. Acid staining is a simple, permanent treatment for cured concrete slabs and can be applied at any time after the concrete has fully cured.

One of the best things about poured concrete is its malleability: in its liquid form, concrete follows curves and angles just as well as straight lines, making it a great medium for custom shapes and sizes.

Walkway molds are filled with poured concrete for easy path or patio construction. The finished product has the appearance of a continuous surface but does not have the same structural properties of a solid concrete walkway.

Loose Materials

Loose materials for patios and walkways encompass a wide range of natural elements, from gravel to wood chips to small river stones. You can use a loose material by itself to create a simple patio or path surface or use it as infill between an arrangement of heavier materials, such as flagstone or large, concrete stepping pavers. In contrast to the solidity and permanence of traditional paving, loose materials have a casual, summery feel. Walking over a pathway of crushed stone or wood chips can feel like a stroll down a country lane or a walk through the woods.

As a primary surface, loose materials offer several practical advantages. They drain well, are forgiving of uneven ground, and can be replenished and graded with a rake for a quick facelift. They also tend to be much less expensive than most other paving options and couldn't be easier to install. In a typical installation, start with a bed of compacted gravel and cover it with landscape fabric to inhibit weed growth and separate the gravel base from the surface material. Then, spread out the surface material a few inches thick, compact it if necessary, and you're done! For simpler applications, such as a lightly traveled garden path, you can often skip the gravel base and lay the landscape fabric right over leveled and tamped soil. In most cases, it's best to include a raised edging of some kind to contain the materials and maintain the shape of the paved surface.

Loose materials can work well on their own or as a complement to surrounding elements. In this landscape, buff-colored gravel serves as both a primary surface and an infill material for a stepping stone path. The natural look of the gravel provides a nice contrast to the formal paver walkway and patio.

Selecting Loose Materials

Because different loose materials can have very different textures and properties, it's important to choose the right surface for the application. Here's a look at some of the most popular materials for patios and walkways:

Decomposed granite: A popular choice for level patios, paths, and driveways, decomposed granite (DG) can be compacted to a relatively smooth, flat, hard surface. DG consists of small pieces of granite ranging in size from sand-size grains to a quarter inch—this size variation is the reason this material is so compactable. DG is available in various natural shades of gray, brown, and tan. Due to its gritty, sandy finish that can stick to your shoes, DG is not a good choice for surfaces that receive heavy traffic directly to and from the house.

Pea gravel and crushed stone: Pea gravel and crushed stone include a broad range of gravel, from fairly fine textures to very coarse. Pea gravel is small- to medium-sized stone that is either mechanically crushed or shaped naturally by water. Crushed stone typically consists of coarse, jagged pieces in various sizes, generally larger than pea gravel. Many types of gravel are compactable, but usually less so than DG. Gravel made up of round stones is more comfortable to walk on than jagged materials.

River rock: Smoothed and rounded by water or machines, river rock ranges from small stones to baseball-sized (and larger) rocks. These smooth surfaces make it more comfortable to walk on than jagged gravel but it is also less compactable and easily displaced underfoot. Larger stones are difficult to walk on and are more suitable for infill and accent areas than for primary paving surfaces.

Wood chips: Wood chips and mulch are commonly used as groundcover in planting beds, gardens, and flowerbeds. Most types are soft and springy underfoot, and many can be used for light-traffic paths and even children's play areas. Wood chips come in a wide variety of grades, colors, and textures. In general, finely chopped and consistent materials are more expensive and more formal in appearance than coarse blends. The term *mulch* is often used interchangeably with wood chips but can also describe roughly chopped wood and other organic matter that's best suited for beds and ground cover. Most loose material made of wood needs some replenishing every two to four years.

Both stone and wood loose materials are typically sold in bulk at landscape and garden centers and by the bag at home centers. Buying in bulk is often much less expensive for all but the smallest jobs. Landscape and garden suppliers typically offer bulk deliveries for a reasonable flat fee. Due to the variance in terminology and appearance of loose materials, be sure to visit the supplier and take a look at the materials you're buying firsthand, so you know exactly what to expect.

Pea gravel

Crushed stone

River rock

Decomposed granite

Wood chips

Tile

With its neat, geometric lines and smooth finish, manufactured tile is a great choice for a formal patio or a nicely appointed front entry. In warm climates, tile is a common outdoor material, often seen in courtyards and fountain plazas paved with large, handmade earthen tiles. In colder regions, outdoor tile must be nearly impervious to water to withstand winter's freeze-thaw cycles. Tile should always be installed over a concrete slab. In fact, this is one of its main uses—the thin profile of most tile makes it a good material for covering a drab, old concrete surface with a fresh, new finish.

Selecting Tile

Indoors, you can use just about any kind of floor tile, but patios are a very different matter. Patio tile must be strong enough to survive scrapes from outdoor furniture as well as years of weather and sun exposure. More importantly, patio tile must be slip-resistant, which automatically rules out most glazed tile. The main types of tile suitable for outdoor use are quarry, terracotta, and porcelain, in addition to natural stone (see page 19).

Quarry tile is a durable ceramic tile that comes unglazed in many colors. It often has a flat but slightly abrasive surface for good slip-resistance.

Terra-cotta tile has a warm, natural appearance, usually in mottled earth tones. It looks great on patios, but because it is somewhat porous, it is not recommended for use in cold climates.

Saltillo tile is a dried, rather than fired, tile similar to terra cotta but with a more imperfect, handmade character. It is also only suitable for mild climates.

Porcelain tile is the toughest, hardest, and often most expensive manufactured tile you can buy. It is highly resistant to water and therefore a good choice for patios in most climates.

When shopping for outdoor tile, be sure to discuss your plans with knowledgeable sales staff. A good tile dealer can help you choose the right type and style of tile for your application and the local climate. They can also help you select appropriate grout and provide maintenance tips for keeping your patio surface in shape throughout the years. Be aware that some tile can discolor or fade over time, due to sun exposure. Sealing grout and, in some cases, tile surfaces are often recommended to prevent staining and to prolong the life of the installation; ask your tile dealer for recommendations.

Tile adds a highly finished look to a patio floor—perfect for an outdoor room with an indoor feel. Like standard floor tile, patio tiles are set into a mortar bed (over a flat concrete slab); then are grouted to complete the job.

Green Materials

As is true for most building projects, installing a new patio or walkway presents a number of environmentally friendly alternatives. One way to go green is to choose paving materials made with recycled components or to use reclaimed materials, such as salvaged brick, reclaimed timbers, or chunks of old concrete. It's also smart to consider how your patio will shed runoff water and how that might affect local flooding zones and waterways.

There are many different options for recycled paving, as well as edging and other landscaping materials. For loose material paving and infill applications, you can buy recycled crushed brick in a range of textures. Pavers made from recycled glass

Using salvaged brick for patios, walkways, or edging is a good application for reusing materials. This yard also forgoes grass for mulch, which saves on water use. The yard is still a lush green due to the hardy vines and low-maintenance shrubs. *Note: Not all salvaged brick is suitable for primary paving surfaces. When setting brick in mortar, be sure to use compatible mortar to prevent cracking.*

are available in several standard sizes for general paving and in large stepping stone sizes. For concrete pavers, look for products made with recycled glass aggregate. Recycled rubber is used in a number of different products, including "paver" patio mats (see pages 121 and 123) and granulated mulch for loose-fill applications and play areas. If you're looking for eco-friendly edging for a patio or path, consider flexible edging and landscape timbers made from recycled plastic.

Permeable paving is an important element of green landscape design for the simple reason that it allows storm water to filter into the ground instead of flowing into municipal drainage systems, where it contributes to flooding problems and contamination of local waterways. Permeable patio and walkway surfaces include sandset pavers and stone, as well as all loose materials, while poured concrete and mortared surfaces are essentially impermeable.

From a green standpoint, impermeable surfaces are fine as long as your patio or walkway is sloped toward an area of natural ground that is large enough to capture and absorb all (or most) seasonal runoff. However, if you have a large paved surface that drains onto another impermeable surface, such as a driveway or street, consider using a permeable paving material instead of solid concrete, or plan for an adequate buffer zone of natural ground between the new surface and other paved areas.

Resources for Green Materials ▸

Recycled-brick loose material (Brick Nuggets): cunninghambrick.com
Glass pavers: environmentalhomecenter.com
Concrete pavers: glass-recycling.com
Rubber patio pavers: gardeners.com
Rubber mulch: americanrubber.com
Plastic landscape edging: mastermark.com
Plastic landscape timbers & lumber: amazingrecycled.com
Permeable pavers: www.belgard.biz/environmental-pavers.htm

To minimize shipping distances from specialty suppliers, search online for a manufacturer near you.

Practical Considerations

In addition to the creative work of planning the look and feel of a patio space, there are several practical matters that must be addressed before you can hit the drawing board. Thinking about how you will use the patio will help you answer one of the biggest questions—how much space you'll need. The planning stage is also the time to consider environmental factors, including site drainage, sunlight, and wind, to make sure your patio will be both comfortable and usable whenever you're ready to get outside. Finally, it's a good idea (and possibly required by law) to check with your city's building department to learn about building code requirements and zoning restrictions that might affect your project plans.

Use

How you plan to spend time on your patio will influence many of your design decisions, so it's best to start the planning process by brainstorming with everyone in your household. What will be the primary uses for the space? Dining, entertaining, sunbathing, playing with the kids, enjoying the view? Once you establish the uses, see if you can accommodate all of those activities within an attractive, efficient design. For some, the solution lies simply in providing adequate space in a flexible floor plan—a quick shift in furniture, for example, can set the stage for the next activity.

In thinking about everything you hope to do on your new patio, imagine the ideal setup for each activity. For example, if you have young children, maybe you want a comfortable sitting area near an edge of the patio that's adjacent to a sandbox (or even a sandbox built into the patio; when the youngest has outgrown it, you can turn it into a planting bed). Or maybe you want some space on the patio for a baby pool or a fountain for the kids to play in.

A patio that's good for entertaining, as well as everyday uses, requires a balanced plan. Large, open areas are best for hosting parties, but can feel empty and overly exposed for a small group of diners. To accommodate both, separate expansive areas from more intimate spaces with a change in floor level or create a more personal, sheltered space by tucking a furniture set into a corner under an arbor. And don't forget to include some personal space: the perfect spot where your favorite chair is always ready for a little reading time or a quick snooze.

Visualizing Your Patio ▶

Create a quick mock-up to help you plan your patio's size, shape, and location. Mark the proposed space with rope or garden hose, and set out any furniture you'll use. See how it all looks from different points on your lot, as well as from inside the house.

If your plan is to refurbish an existing patio, think hard about what you like and dislike about the current setup. A patio that's too small can be expanded along its borders or can be connected with a walkway to a new, separate patio space designed for other uses. Often patios don't get used because they're uncomfortable or uninviting during free time. For example, if you get home from work just as the western sun is blasting the area with heat, you'll probably stay inside. The solution is a simple shade barrier that blocks those afternoon rays.

Size & Layout

The ideal size and configuration for your patio is determined by the space needed for each activity, including plenty of room for easy access and intervening traffic. With the floor space allocated, you can begin playing around with different layouts, design elements, and shapes until the form of the space complements all of its functions. All the while, keep the big picture in mind—make sure the proportions and general design of the patio complement your house and the rest of the landscape.

How Much Space?

Time to think again about all the uses you have planned for the patio. If you already have the patio furniture, set it up on the proposed site and experiment with different arrangements to get a sense of how much space each furniture grouping will need. If you don't have the furniture yet, see the illustration below for suggestions on spacing. Next, decide which areas you want to be dedicated for specific activities and which can be rearranged for multiple uses. Cooking and dining areas are best as static, or *anchored*, stations, while an informal sunbathing spot defined by a couple of lounge chairs can easily be rearranged or moved as needed.

To plan traffic routes, allow a minimum of 22" of width for main passages between and alongside activity areas (32" minimum for wheelchair access). The main goal is having enough room for people to move around the patio without disrupting any activities.

Take a Step Back

As your patio plans develop, try to envision the design within its context. Does the size seem appropriate for the house and lot? How do the size and layout translate to atmosphere? While it's important to make a patio large enough for all its intended uses, there's also a risk in making it too large. With interior rooms, some people like the grandeur and openness of a sprawling great room with a cathedral ceiling, while others find the expansive space uncomfortable for personal activities like reading or quiet conversation.

Architects often design in terms of "human scale," creating spaces that are large enough to accommodate the human body in its everyday activities but small enough to provide a comfortable sense of space and enclosure. On a patio, you can establish the proper scale with clear barriers, such as fences and overheads, or with boundaries that rely more on perception—low walls, plantings, or even just a change in flooring materials.

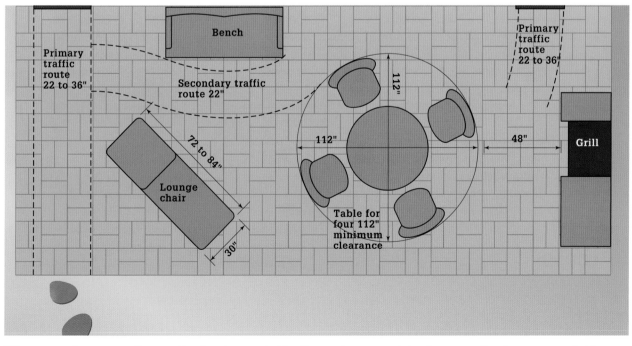

When arranging your patio, consider the placement of furniture and permanent structures as well as the space needed for primary traffic routes. These routes should have a minimum width of 22" to allow for comfortable passage throughout the patio.

Zoning Laws, Building Codes & Utilities

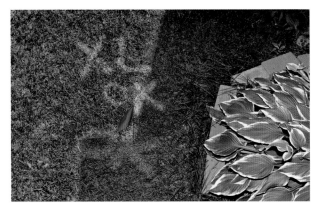

Contact local utility companies to have all utility lines marked on your property. This is necessary before digging in your yard, and it could affect your patio location. Utility companies promptly send out a representative to mark the lines.

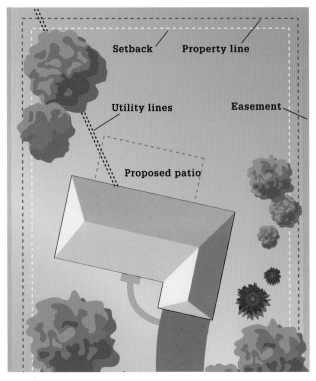

Always check your municipality's zoning laws when planning a new patio project.

Any alterations made to your lot could fall under your municipality's zoning laws. In the case of a new patio, zoning laws might limit locations for the patio and how much ground it can cover. The latter relates to the allowable percentage of development on the lot (adding a large patio now could preclude future plans for a home addition). Also make sure the patio conforms to setback restrictions (required distance from lot lines) and easements (zones that must be accessible for utilities and other public services). Walls, fire features, or overhead structures may be subject to standards set by the local building codes, and you may need to obtain building permits.

Discuss your complete plans with an official at the local municipality's planning office for zoning laws. If you run into snags, ask about alternatives; for example, a poured concrete patio may not be allowed over an easement, but a less permanent, sandset surface may be approved.

Also, contact the local utility companies to have all utility lines marked on your property. Most states are part of the North American One Call Referral System (888-258-0808), which will contact all of the utilities in your area to have lines in your yard marked.

Access

Like most recreation and relaxation areas, a patio tends to be used more often if it's easily accessible. The same is true of visual access. Full views, or even just glimpses, of the patio from several interior rooms will beckon you outdoors on nice days.

Another important consideration involves the rooms that lead to the patio. For example, if outdoor dining is one of your primary activities, locating the patio near the kitchen will prove to be an enormous convenience. Similarly, a patio used frequently for large parties should not be accessed through a bedroom or other private space. This is not only an inconvenience, guests feel uncomfortable walking through private or formal areas of a home.

Atmosphere

Perhaps the most important elements of all are the everyday factors that affect the quality of life on a patio, including sunlight, noise, privacy, and views. Does the site get enough sunlight (or too much) at the times you're most likely to use it? Are noise levels acceptable—or will you need to put up a fence? Will you feel overly exposed and on display, or too shut in? Finally, what you see from the patio has a big impact on the atmosphere. If there are no good views available, add landscaping, plants, or decorations to create a pleasant view.

Dealing with Drainage

It's not unusual that a new patio creates, or is subject to, drainage problems. One common cause is a hard paved surface that sheds water instead of absorbing it and deposits it along the lower edge of the patio. There, the water collects, creating a swampy area of grass. During heavy rains, runoff water can build up enough force to wash out flower beds bordering a patio. Drainage problems can also occur when the water has no escape, a common condition with sunken or recessed patios that are surrounded by retaining walls or ascending slopes. Additionally, adding or removing soil or plants to make room for a patio can alter natural drainage patterns, potentially resulting in an unpleasant surprise with the first good rain.

Fortunately, all of these problems can be solved with an appropriate drainage system. For patio runoff, a drainage swale or perimeter trench is usually effective. These are sloped channels or trenches that collect excess groundwater and divert it to a collection point. A trench running along the lowest edge of the patio can collect water directly from the patio surface. If the patio is at the top of a natural slope leading to a low point in the yard, a drainage swale located in the low point keeps the rest of the yard relatively dry.

Diverting excess water is only half of the battle—the water also needs a place to go. Ideally, it is collected on your property, where it filters through the soil and returns to natural aquifers. This can be achieved with a dry well (see pages 49 to 50) or with a swale leading to a natural collection area in the landscape (see pages 46 to 48). Another option is to divert excess runoff to a street gutter or a storm drain, but this design must be approved by the city's planning department. For further discussion on surface drainage and environmental considerations, see page 25.

Enclosed or recessed patios may require their own drainage system, typically with some type of floor drain. The patio surface slopes toward the drain, located either in the center or along one side, where runoff water collects in a subsurface catch basin. From there, an underground drainpipe carries the water to a collection point. If you think your patio will need this type of system, consult an engineer or qualified landscape professional early in the planning process to discuss your options.

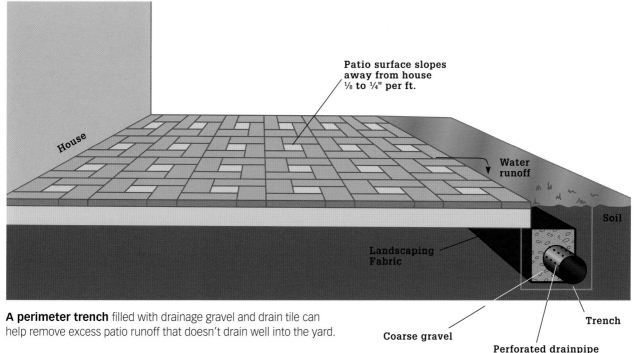

Patio surface slopes away from house ⅛ to ¼" per ft.

House

Water runoff

Soil

Landscaping Fabric

Coarse gravel

Trench

Perforated drainpipe (drain tile) slopes ¼" per ft. toward collection point

A perimeter trench filled with drainage gravel and drain tile can help remove excess patio runoff that doesn't drain well into the yard.

Climate Control

Careful planning can't change the weather, but it can help you make the best of prevailing conditions. By controlling or using sunlight and shade, wind, and natural air currents, you can make your patio the most comfortable place in your outdoor landscape. Consider the following:

Sunlight and shadows: The unalterable pattern of the sun is one of the few climatic systems you can count on. The tricky part is positioning your patio so it receives the right amount and intensity of sunlight at the time of day—and the season—when you'll use it most. Remember that the sun's path changes throughout the year. In summer, it rises high in the sky along the east-west axis, creating shorter shadows and more exposure overall. In winter, the sun's angle is relatively low, resulting in long shadows in the northwest, north, and northeast directions. To avoid shadows altogether, locate your patio away from the house and other structures.

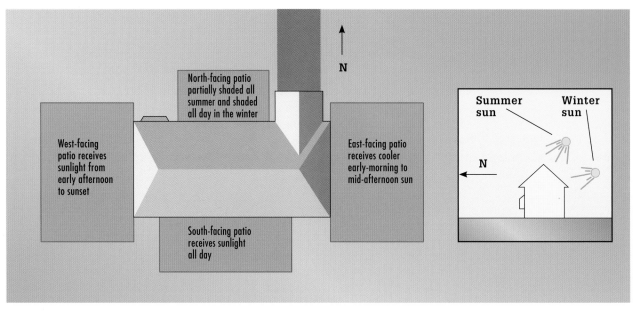

Remember to consider the amount of sunlight your patio will receive to make sure your planned project will meet your needs.

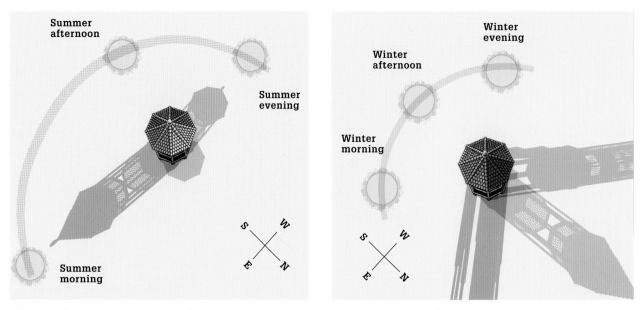

Shadows follow the east-west axis in the summer.

Winter shadows point to the northeast and northwest and are relatively long at midday.

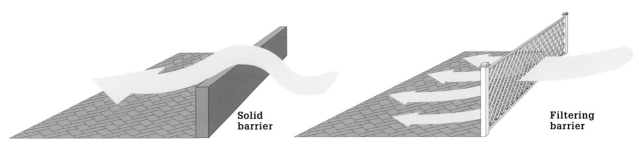

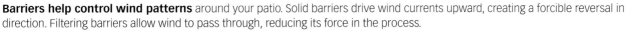

Solid
barrier

Filtering
barrier

Barriers help control wind patterns around your patio. Solid barriers drive wind currents upward, creating a forcible reversal in direction. Filtering barriers allow wind to pass through, reducing its force in the process.

Wind currents can ruin your patio peace as surely as a rainstorm. Shielding yourself from wind takes careful planning and sometimes trial and error. Since you can't protect against all wind, first determine the direction of prevailing winds—the most frequent and strongest wind currents affecting your site (prevailing winds may change with the seasons)—then decide on the best location for a wind barrier. Contrary to appearances, a solid barrier often is not the most effective windbreak; these barriers force air currents to swoop over the top and then drop down on the backside, returning to full strength at a distance roughly equal to the barrier's height. A more reliable windbreak is created with a lattice or louvered fence that diffuses and weakens the wind as it passes through the barrier.

Patio materials and orientation: The surface material you choose can also affect the patio environment. Dark-colored, solid surfaces—like brick or dark stone—absorb a lot of heat during the day and may become uncomfortable to walk on in sunny areas. However, after the sun goes down, stored heat released from the paving can warm the air on the patio. Solid walls also reflect heat and can restrict cooling breezes. Because cold air sinks, low-lying patios or those positioned at the base of an incline tend to be cooler than higher areas of the landscape.

If you're building an overhead specifically for shade, experiment with alternative materials, such as bamboo screening or fabric, to filter sunlight and control wind.

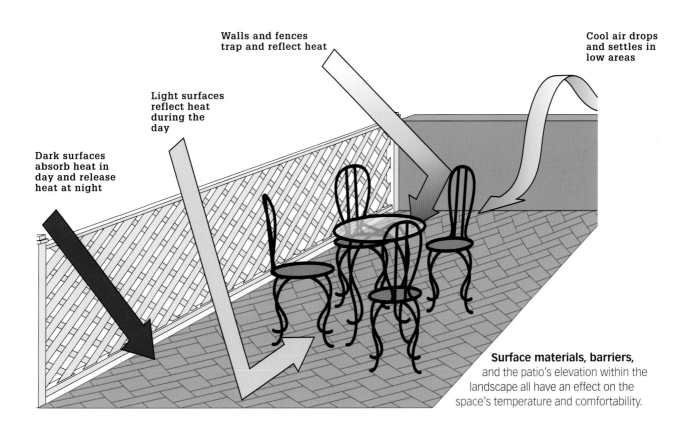

Walls and fences
trap and reflect heat

Cool air drops
and settles in
low areas

Light surfaces
reflect heat
during the
day

Dark surfaces
absorb heat in
day and release
heat at night

Surface materials, barriers,
and the patio's elevation within the
landscape all have an effect on the
space's temperature and comfortability.

Patio & Walkway Plans

This section offers a different kind of inspiration from the section on design themes. Here you'll see detailed patio and landscape plans for several different types of properties, each showing specific design solutions for making the most of the available space and existing conditions. One or more of the properties might resemble your own, but even if none of them does, don't worry; the idea is to see how various elements can be put to use and to think about how some of those solutions might work in your own plan.

The five designs, starting on the following page, are shown in *plan*, or aerial, view. This is the perspective that professionals use to do much of their design work, as it provides not only a bird's-eye view of the entire site, it's also the best way to see how the patio, walkways, and other elements relate to the house and surrounding landscape. Plan drawings of your own property can be quite helpful in designing and planning a new patio or path project (see below).

Drawing Your Own Plans ▸

Unless you need them for getting a permit or other official business, detailed drawings of your site and new projects are optional. But there are a few good reasons to map out your property and at least sketch your basic plans onto paper. Scaled drawings are good for showing relationships between elements and overall proportions within a plan, and are helpful for estimating materials and making shopping lists. If you hire out any of the work, detailed drawings will be invaluable for obtaining accurate bids and to help you keep the project on track during construction. Also, sketches are always useful for conveying or experimenting with ideas.

When making your own drawings, it's best to work from a base map, or site plan—an aerial view of the project site and as much of the surrounding area as is relevant. The site plan should include:

- The house (at least the wall adjacent to the patio), including doors, windows, and light fixtures
- Trees, significant plantings, and other landscaping features
- Gutter downspouts, outdoor faucets, and electrical outlets
- Notes about prevailing winds, lot grading (for sloping sites), and natural drainage routes
- Views (good and bad) from the patio site
- Sun and wind patterns

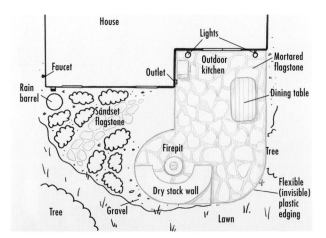

An accurately scaled site plan puts your property into perspective and helps you think like a designer. Create a plan using your own measurements or locate the plat map or original blueprints of your property (check with the local city or county planning offices or your mortgage/title company).

Sketch your designs onto clean copies of the site plan, or use an overlay of tracing paper for each new drawing. As you refine your plans, create more detailed, smaller-scale drawings of the patio/walkway site and immediate surroundings.

Sample Patio Plan 1

Like most lots in established urban neighborhoods, this back yard space was short on both space and privacy. But by devoting most of the area to two patios and the rest to planting beds, this design provides ample room for entertaining, outdoor dining, and even gardening.

The main patio space is paved with cut stone for a natural yet clean look and a smooth surface that's good for nighttime parties and frequent traffic between the house and the back gate. In one corner, a flagstone coffee table and fountain define a casual "lounge" area; the fountain also helps dampen the city's noise. A vine-covered arbor (or trellis) provides shade and privacy for half of the lounge area and a portion of the smaller planting bed.

Opposite the lounge area, a cozy corner patio is the perfect stage for intimate gatherings and everyday meals. Its natural flagstone floor is two short steps up from the main patio surface. This, along with the decorative post-and-beam gate, gives the dining space a special, secluded feel. A fan-shaped arbor could be added here for shade and more privacy.

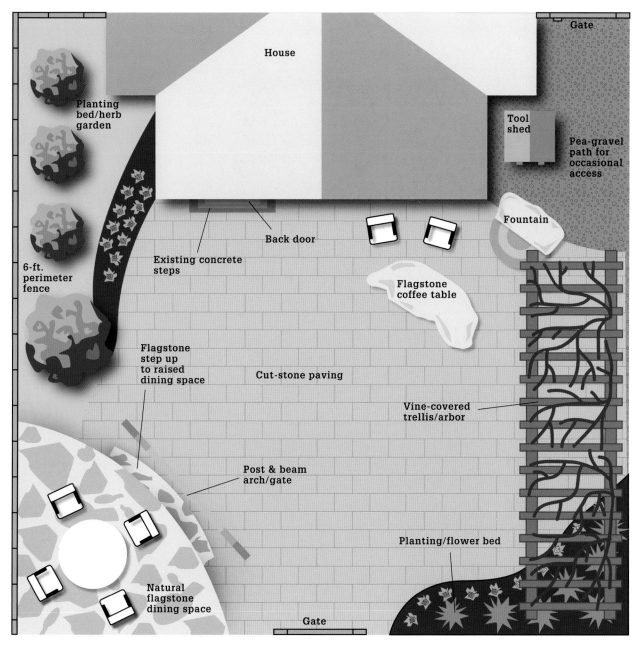

This multifunctional design adds privacy while creating multiple spaces for entertaining.

Sample Patio Plan 2

Sloping ground can be a challenge for patio plans, but can also be an opportunity for creating dramatic features or perspectives you can't get with a flat surface. In this back yard site, the area near the middle of the house was relatively close to grade. Adding a few retaining walls allowed the patio to extend out to both sides. One retaining wall cuts into the slope along the south end of the site, providing space and a boundary for a paver walkway linking the patio to the front yard. This abuts a four-foot-tall masonry wall that carves a 90-degree space into the slope and provides a backdrop (and backsplash) for an L-shaped outdoor kitchen.

The low wall at the north end of the patio retains earth for the patio surface and helps create a lofty feel for the sitting area outside the home's master bedroom. A planter with trees provides a subtle barrier between the sitting area and the main patio space. Out on the yard's planted slope, a set of stone steps leads to gently climbing stepping stone paths laid out for either strolling through the foliage or tending to garden plants.

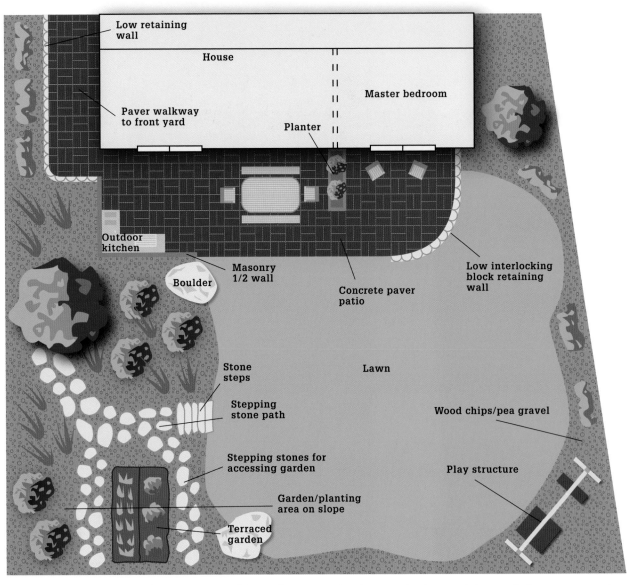

To make the most of a sloping yard, use retaining walls, steps, and paths to emphasize grand views and allow easy access to garden areas.

Sample Patio Plan 3

This grand design, created for a large suburban or rural property, has a setting for every mood and occasion: the expansive brick patio provides an elegant venue for both formal and casual entertaining. Guests (and kids) will feel more than welcome to step out onto the lawn for back yard games or a stroll through the grounds.

In addition to its ample open space, the brick patio serves as an entryway to a screened porch—a welcome retreat for hot, wet, or buggy weather. At the other end, the patio surrounds a small sun deck designed for a few lounge chairs or perhaps a bistro set used for drinks or everyday meals.

Away from the main patio, two destinations offer getaways of distinctly different character: follow the pebbled stepping-stone path through the archway to the sun-sheltered garden view from the gazebo. Or, stroll across the lawn after dark for stargazing around the open fire on the circular gravel patio.

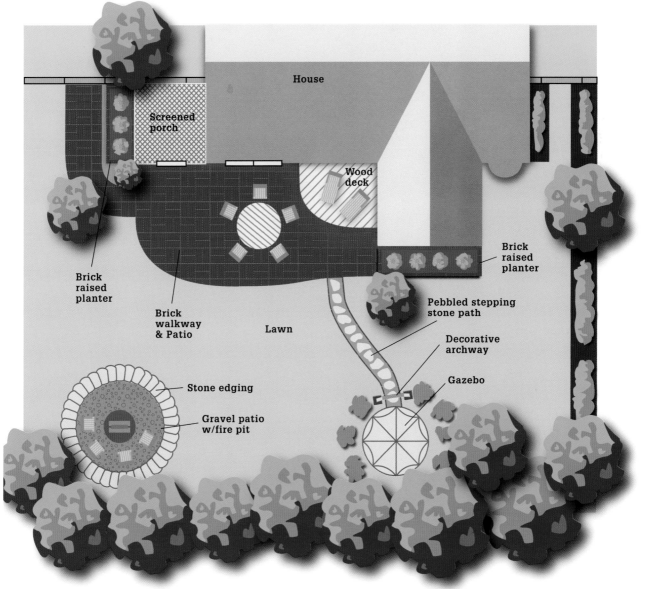

This design provides outdoor rooms for all purposes—gathering around a fire, dining, sunbathing, relaxing in a screened-in porch, or enjoying the view from a gazebo.

Sample Patio Plan 4

Casual and organic in feel, this plan with sandset flagstone surfaces embodies the spirit of the ranch home, in which the patio is used as an extension of the indoor spaces. Running the full length of the home, the patio is accessible from several different rooms and is likewise visible from each.

An arbor with vine-covered trellis screen defines and shelters a dining space located just outside of the home's kitchen. And for the cook, a large planting bed adjacent to the patio provides easy access to fresh herbs, fruits, and vegetables. An integrated sandbox keeps the kids near the house and out of the hot afternoon sun. Both the sandbox and integrated flowerbed are simply excavated areas filled with play sand over soil and landscape fabric.

In keeping with the natural look of the patio paving, flagstones are used for a well-traveled walkway between the front and back yards, while a compacted gravel path with natural stone edging creates an attractive service road leading from the shed to the back garden.

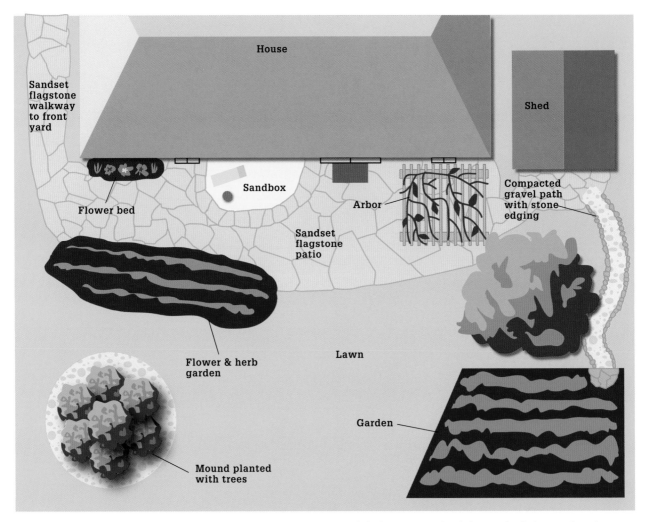

This sandset flagstone patio is accessible from multiple areas around the house, seamlessly integrating indoor and outdoor living.

Sample Patio Plan 5

This new suburban property presented a challenge to the standard patio plan: the back of the house seemed just right for a full-sized patio, but the neighboring property was so close that the view from the patio would be dominated by the neighbor's kitchen (and *their* back yard patio). The better view was from the front of the house. Therefore, this design places the main patio space around the front door, incorporating the existing entry stoop and portico. A second, smaller patio made with circular concrete pavers serves as a landing and casual sitting area just outside the patio door leading to the back yard.

Because it faces the street, is well-integrated with the house, and is partially sheltered with overheads, the entry patio feels a lot like a traditional front porch. A low masonry wall adds definition and a sense of enclosure to the patio. However, to maintain a welcoming feel for the front entry, a large opening in the wall leaves plenty of room for the existing concrete walkway. Also, the walkway remains uninterrupted from the sidewalk to the front stoop, clearly indicating the direct route to the front door. The patio paving is level with the walkway so the entire space is useable as a patio surface when needed.

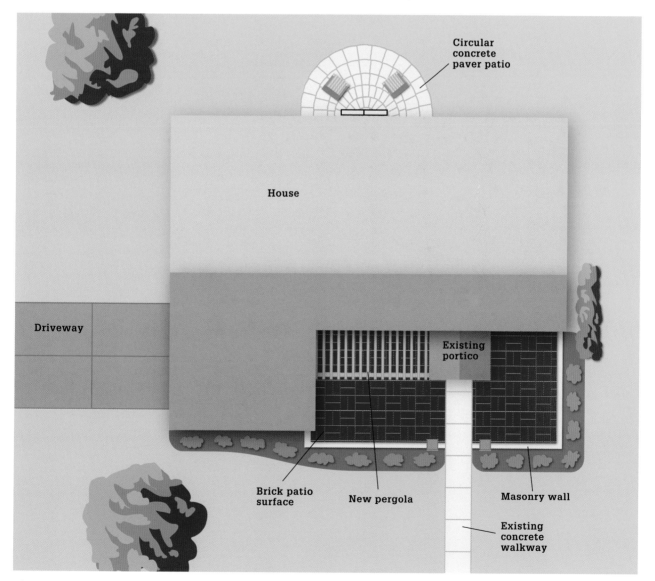

Circular concrete paver patio

House

Driveway

Existing portico

Brick patio surface

New pergola

Masonry wall

Existing concrete walkway

If the best view of your home is in the front, consider constructing a landscaped patio around your home's existing entryway, as shown in this design. A small patio in back is still a practical addition for greater privacy.

Patio Projects

Time to break ground. This chapter covers all of the most popular patio materials in complete step-by-step projects. You'll also find a few projects for taking care of specific site challenges, such as drainage and sloping ground, before getting started on the patio construction. When you're ready to begin your paving project, be sure to read the Layout & Surface Preparation section on pages 40 to 45. This includes detailed steps for setting up reference lines and creating a stable foundation for any type of patio surface.

If you're still weighing your options with different patio materials, consider ease of installation: the fastest and easiest patios to build are those made with loose materials. Next are sandset surfaces that require careful planning and layout, but it's relatively easy to correct mistakes. With mortared surfaces, you're working against the clock to get everything set and cleaned up before the mortar hardens, and mistakes are tough to fix. Poured concrete is the most challenging material, due to the time sensitivity and the finer points of finishing.

In this chapter:

Layout & Surface Preparation

The first major step of any patio project is to set up guide strings. Once that's finished, excavation begins and then a layer of gravel is added. The gravel is an essential element of patio construction: like your house's foundation, it creates a flat, stable base for building upon; and it protects the surface material by providing drainage underneath to minimize shifting and settling caused by seasonal freeze-thaw cycles.

There are a few matters to take care of before you begin the layout and surface prep work. The first is to determine the thickness of each layer of the patio construction. This includes the thicknesses of the surface material, the sand bed (if required), and the gravel subbase. For most patio types, the gravel layer should be four inches thick (after compaction). Concrete slab patios call for six inches of gravel, but this is subject to the local building code and may vary by region. The combined thicknesses of the layers minus the distance the patio surface will stand above the ground gives you the depth of the excavation.

The height of the finished patio aboveground is up to you. The standard minimum height is one inch. This ensures the patio will drain properly, but it's low enough to cut any bordering grass with a mower.

The next factor to determine is the total drop distance—the change in elevation from the high end to the low end of the patio surface. This creates the slope necessary for water runoff. Your patio should slope away from the house foundation or other adjacent structure (and preferably away from main traffic routes) at a rate of ⅛" per linear foot. For example, if your patio will extend 12" from your house, the drop distance of the patio surface will be 1½". In the following project, you'll calculate the drop distance by measuring from the house (or high edge of the patio) to the batterboards at the low edge. The batterboards are set about 12" beyond the finished patio edges, and this additional amount makes the final drop distance more accurate than using the finished patio dimensions.

The final step before you start digging is to locate underground utility lines in the project site. Call your utility service providers or a national provider (see Resources, page 250) to have your lines marked.

Tools & Materials ▶

Drill	Lumber (2 × 2,
Circular saw	2 × 4)
Hammer	2½" coarse-thread
Level	drywall screws
Hand maul	Common nails
Mason's string	Compactable gravel
Line level	Eye and ear
Power sod cutter or	protection
lawn edger	Work gloves
Excavation tools	Rope or garden hose
Bow rake	Marking paint
Plate compactor or	Flat spade
hand tamp	U-shaped wire
Shovel	stakes (optional)
Wheelbarrow	Landscape fabric
Plumb bob	(optional)

Set up batterboards for the layout strings to easily remove and replace strings without losing the slope and layout settings. A story pole—measured against temporary cross strings—makes it easy to check the depth of each layer as you work. Remember to call utility companies to have them mark utility lines in or near the project site before excavating.

How to Prepare & Excavate a Patio Site

Construct the batterboards from 2 × 4 lumber and 2½" screws: cut the batterboard legs 24" long, and then taper the ends to a point. Cut the cross-pieces at 24". Align and fasten the legs perpendicular to the ends of the cross-pieces. Use a nail or screw at the top center of each crosspiece.

Roughly mark the patio corners with 2 × 2 stakes. Cut the 2 × 2 ends to a taper (the greater the angle, the easier it will be to drive into the ground). Tap the tapered end into the ground with a hand maul or sledgehammer.

Drive pairs of batterboards about 2 ft. behind the stakes, holding them plumb and level. The tops of the crosspieces should be about 12" above the ground. If the patio abuts the house, drive a single 2 × 4 stake at each corner so one face of the stake is even with the planned edge of the patio.

Tie a mason's string taut between an outer batterboard nail and one of the house-side (or high edge of the patio) stakes. Attach a line level (inset) to the string and adjust the stakes as needed until the string is perfectly level.

Begin setting the slope on the first layout string: stand the pole next to the batterboard and mark the height of the level mason's string. Measure between the house (or high side) stake to the batterboard, then calculate the drop distance for the string—a common slope is ¼" per linear foot.

(continued)

Using the story pole as a guide, drive the batterboard down until the string is even with the drop distance mark. Make sure the crosspiece remains level across the top so the string's height won't change if you move the string later.

Set up the remaining three string lines so they are even with the outer edges of the finished patio and are just touching the first string. First install the two strings parallel to the house, and use the line level to confirm they are level. The final string (parallel to the first string) will have the proper slope when it touches the intersecting strings.

Variation: Use a rope or a garden hose to lay out curved or freeform patio edges. Mark the outline onto the ground with marking paint. Once you complete the subbase, you can repeat the process to guide the installation. *Note: Curving patios still need a string layout to guide the excavation and base prep.*

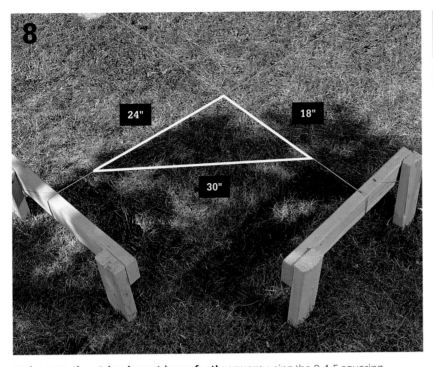

8

24"

18"

30"

Checking for Square ▸

The traditional 3-4-5 technique can also be used for larger multiples of 3, 4, and 5. This provides greater accuracy for larger patios. For example, use 6, 8, and 10 ft.

Alternatively, you can use a long tape to measure between opposing corners of the layout. When the measurements are equal, the layout is square.

Make sure the string layout is perfectly square using the 3-4-5 squaring technique: starting at one of the string intersections, measure along one string and make a mark at 3 ft. (or a multiple of 3 ft.). Measure along the perpendicular string and mark at 4 ft. Measure between the two marks: the distance should equal 5 ft. If not, adjust the strings as needed until the measurements come out correctly. Repeat the process at the diagonally opposed corner. Mark the string positions onto the batterboard crosspieces.

9

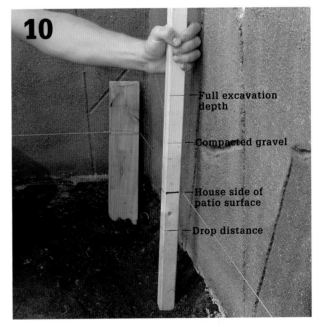

10

- Full excavation depth
- Compacted gravel
- House side of patio surface
- Drop distance

Determine the finished height of the patio surface. If the patio abuts the house, the finished surface should be 1 to 3" below the typical threshold of an entry door. At the low end of the patio it's desirable to have the finished surface rise at least 1" above the surrounding ground to facilitate drainage and prevent dirt and mud from washing onto the patio.

On your story pole, mark a top line for the distance from the string line (measured at the high edge of the patio) to the full excavation depth. A second line represents the distance from the string to the top of the compacted gravel base. Be sure to account for the thickness of the paving material and sand bed as needed.

(continued)

Cut the sod along the project outline using a flat-end spade or a power lawn edger. To compensate for edging, extend the excavation about 6" beyond the finished patio outline. Reserve healthy sod for covering soil backfill behind the edging.

Strip the sod or vegetation inside the outlined area and then excavate the construction area to a depth that allows for a 6"-thick gravel subbase, a 1" layer of sand, and the paver thickness; account for the finished height aboveground also.

Grade and compact the soil. First use a bow rake to achieve the proper slope, and then compact the soil with a rented plate or hand tamper. Set up temporary cross strings for reference to simplify the excavation and the gravel installation later.

Depth stake

Use the story pole to check the depth as you work. Drive a pair of 2 × 2 stakes outside of the original string layout, and tie on the cross string so it's just touching the layout strings. Check the depth at several points along the cross string, removing or adding soil as needed to achieve the proper depth. Once that's done, move the cross string to the next section and repeat. *Note: Thoroughly tamp any soil that's been added to a low spot to minimize future settling. For the same reason, it's best to use soil from the immediate area (instead of purchased topsoil) or fill low areas with compacted sand or gravel.*

Variation: For loose-fill patios, install a layer of high-quality landscape fabric to inhibit weed growth before adding the gravel base. Overlap rows of fabric by at least 6". If desired, pin the fabric in place with U-shaped wire stakes.

Add the first layer of compactable gravel (or start with landscape fabric; see Variation this page). Dump wheelbarrow loads of gravel into evenly distributed pods, then spread out each pod in all directions with a shovel and a bow rake. Use the rake to create a flat, smooth surface.

Thoroughly tamp each layer of gravel before adding more, as needed. If using a hand tamper, compact the gravel in 2"-thick layers; if using a plate compactor, compact every 4" of gravel. Use cross strings and the story pole to check the gravel height as you work. A straight 2 × 4 also helps for smoothing gravel prior to compacting and for checking for high and low spots.

Extend a plumb bob from the layout strings to the base to mark the exact corners and edges of the finished patio for the surface installation. Mark each point with paint or a small stake. Find and mark the corners of the patio by hanging the plumb bob from each string intersection. Proceed to the installation portion of your project.

Drainage Swales

If your new patio area may potentially collect rainwater or is sloped in such a way that runoff water flows into unwanted places, you will need to improve or redirect the drainage of the area. One effective way to do this is to create a swale.

A swale is a shallow ditch that carries water away from the yard to a designated collection area, usually a gutter, sewer catch bin, stream, or lake. Most communities restrict the redirecting of runoff water, so always contact your local inspector's office to discuss your plans before you begin.

If you're building a swale between your house and the neighboring yard, talk to your neighbor about the project before you begin. If drainage is a problem in their yard as well, they may be willing to share the expense and the work of the project.

Building a swale is relatively simple, but it involves the labor of digging a trench. We'll show you how to construct the swale using a shovel, but for larger swales, you'll want to rent a trencher or backhoe. If you decide to use a trencher or backhoe, you'll still need to use a shovel to create the V shape and to smooth the sides of the trench.

Tools & Materials ▶

Hammer or maul	Landscape fabric
Wheelbarrow	Rough gravel
Spade	Shovel
Sod cutter (optional)	Work gloves
Stakes	

Runoff direction

Drainage swale

Improve drainage in a large low-lying area by creating a shallow ditch, called a drainage swale, to carry runoff water away. If your region receives frequent heavy rainfalls or if you have dense soil that drains poorly, you may need to lay a perforated drainpipe and a bed of gravel under the swale to make it more effective (see page 48).

How to Build a Drainage Swale

After identifying the problem area, use stakes to mark a swale route that will direct water away from the site toward a runoff area. The outlet of the swale should be lower than any other point in the problem area whenever possible.

Dig a 6"-deep trench along the swale route. If you remove the sod carefully, you can lay it back into the trench when the swale is completed.

Shape the trench so it slopes gradually downward toward the outlet, and the sides and bottom are smooth.

Complete the swale by laying sod into the trench. Compress the sod, and then water the area thoroughly to check drainage.

Swale Options

Coarse gravel

Perforated drain pipe

Splash block

For severe drainage problems, dig a 1-ft.-deep swale angled slightly downward to the outlet point. Line the swale with landscape fabric. Spread a 2"-layer of coarse gravel in the bottom of the swale, and then lay perforated drainpipe over the gravel. Cover the pipe with a 5"-layer of gravel, then wrap the landscape fabric over the top of the gravel. Cover the swale with soil and fresh sod. Set a splash block at the outlet to distribute the runoff and prevent erosion.

Types of Gravel ▸

Rough

Smooth

Gravel comes in two forms: rough and smooth. When buying gravel for shaping projects, such as drainage swales, select rough gravel. Rough gravel clings to the sides of the trench, creating an even drainage layer. Smooth gravel is typically used as a decorative ground cover. When used for shaping projects, it tends to slide toward the middle of the trench.

Dry Wells

Downspouts and other house drainage systems are common obstacles for new patio projects. The problem is simple: the water needs a place to go. Sometimes downspouts can be extended or repositioned to clear the patio area, and natural drainage routes in your yard can be altered with a swale. But often the best solution is to capture the water and divert it to a dry well in your yard.

A dry well system typically consists of a buried drain tile running from a catch basin at the water source to a collection container some distance away. A basic system is easy and inexpensive to install. In the project shown here, a perforated plastic drain tile connects to a dry well fashioned from a plastic trash can that has been drilled with holes and then filled with stone rubble. Water can percolate into the soil as it makes its way along the drainpipe, while the well serves as a large collection area that drains excess water slowly into the surrounding earth.

Tools & Materials ›

Hammer or maul
Wheelbarrow
Spade
Mason's string
Line level
Tape measure
Jigsaw
Drill and 1" bit
Stakes

Landscape fabric
Gravel
Plastic trash can
Perforated drain tile
Large stones
Catch basin
Eye and ear
  protection
Work gloves

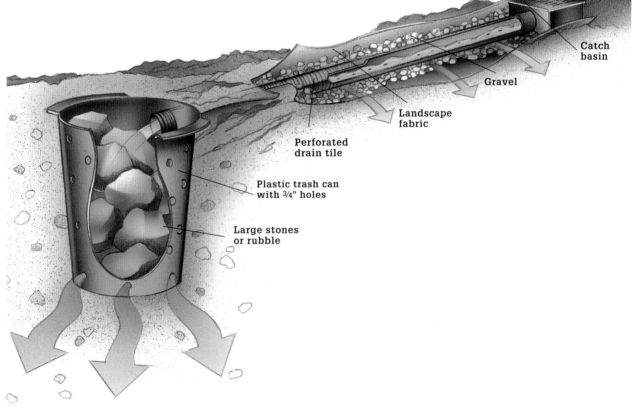

Catch basin

Gravel

Landscape fabric

Perforated drain tile

Plastic trash can with ¾" holes

Large stones or rubble

A dry well helps divert runoff water away from your patio and into the ground a distance from your home.

How to Install a Dry Well

Excavate a 10"-wide by 14"-deep trench along the planned route from the catch basin to the dry well. Line the hole and trench with landscape fabric. Fold the excess over the sides of the trench and hole.

Lay a 1"-layer of gravel on the bottom of the trench. Place the drain tile in the trench. Trace the outline of the drain tile onto the trash can side, 3" from the top. Cut a hole in the trash can along the outline using a jigsaw. Use a drill with a 1" bit to drill drainage holes through the sides and bottom of the can every 4 to 6".

Place the can in the hole, run the drain tile 2" into the side of the can, and fill the can with large rocks. Check the slope of the drain tile with a level, adjusting the layer of gravel below, if necessary.

Connect the catch basin in the problem area. Position it so the excess water will flow directly into it. Fill the trench with gravel, 1" over the drain tile.

Fold the landscape fabric edges over the gravel and fill the trench with the soil you removed earlier. Replace the sod in the trench area. Water the area thoroughly.

Retaining Walls

A sloping yard often means limited space for a patio. And while a steeply sloping patio might seem like fun to the kids, it would be decidedly inconvenient for dinner parties. The answer, then, is to build retaining walls. Retaining walls cut into a slope (and in some cases, replace the slope), bridging the upper and lower levels while adding more useable area to both.

Low retaining walls can be built with a variety of materials, including landscape timbers and natural stone. But by far the most popular material for do-it-yourself projects is interlocking concrete block made specifically for retaining walls. This block requires no mortar—most types are simply stacked in ordered rows—and it has flanges or pins that automatically set the batter for the wall (the backward lean that most retaining walls have for added strength). Interlocking block is available at home and garden centers and landscape suppliers. Most blocks have roughly textured faces. You'll need standard blocks, corner blocks, and cap stones.

Due to the structural factors involved, the recommended height limit for do-it-yourself retaining walls is three feet. Anything higher is best left to a professional. Retaining walls of any size may be governed by the local building code; contact your city's building department to learn about construction specifications and permit requirements.

Tools & Materials ▸

Excavation tools	Compactable gravel
Mason's string	Interlocking
Line level	concrete block
Tape measure	Crushed stone
Hand tamper	Perforated drainpipe
Plate compactor	Construction
Circular saw with	adhesive (and
masonry blade	caulk gun)
Maul	Flour or marking
Chisel	paint
Level	Eye and ear
Stakes	protection
Professional-grade	Work gloves
landscape fabric	

Shaping Your Site with Retaining Walls ▸

Shown here are two methods of reshaping the same natural slope. In the top photo, the retaining wall is placed at the bottom of the original slope. Extra soil is brought in to fill behind the wall, thus creating more level land on top. In the bottom photo, the wall divides the original slope. Soil cut from the base of the hill is reused as fill behind the top of the wall. The result is a newly controlled area for building a patio below the wall, as well as a modest gain of level ground above.

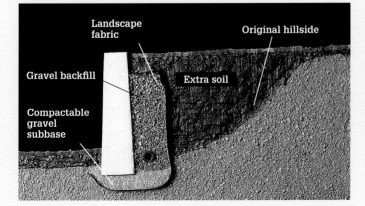

Landscape fabric — Original hillside — Gravel backfill — Extra soil — Compactable gravel subbase

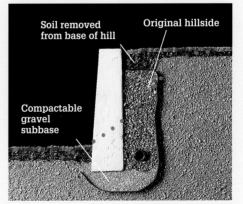

Soil removed from base of hill — Original hillside — Compactable gravel subbase

How to Build a Retaining Wall with Interlocking Concrete Block

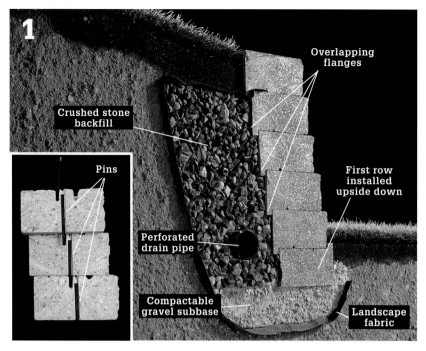

Interlocking wall blocks do not need mortar. Some types are held together with a system of overlapping flanges that automatically set the backward pitch (batter) as the blocks are stacked, as shown in this project. Other types of blocks use fiberglass pins (inset).

Excavate the hillside, if necessary. Allow 12" of space for the crushed stone backfill between the back of the wall and the hill side. Use stakes to mark the front edge of the wall. Connect the stakes with mason's string and use a line level to check for level.

Dig out the bottom of the excavation below ground level so it is 6" lower than the height of the block. For example, if you use 6"-thick block, dig down 12". Measure down from the string to make sure the bottom base is level.

Line the excavation with strips of landscape fabric cut 3 ft. longer than the planned height of the wall. Make sure all seams overlap by at least 6".

5

Spread a 6"-layer of compactable gravel over the bottom of the excavation as a subbase and pack it thoroughly. A rented plate compactor works better than a hand tamper for packing the subbase.

6

Lay the first course of block, aligning the front edges with the mason's string. When using flanged block, place the first course upside down and backward. Frequently check for level and adjust, if necessary, by adding or removing subbase material below the blocks.

7

Drainage gravel

Second course

Level line

First course

Lay the second course of block according to manufacturer's instructions, checking to make sure the blocks are level. Lay flanged block with the flanges tight against the underlying course. Add 3 to 4" of gravel behind the block, and pack it with a hand tamper.

8

Make half-blocks for the corners and ends of a wall, and use them to stagger vertical joints between courses. Score full blocks with a circular saw and masonry blade, then break the blocks along the scored line with a maul and chisel. Some manufacturers make corner blocks available.

(continued)

Add and tamp crushed stone, as needed, to create a slight downward pitch—about ¼" of height per foot of pipe—leading to the drainpipe outlet. Place the drain pipe on the crushed stone, 6" behind the wall, with the perforations face down. Make sure the pipe outlet is unobstructed. Lay courses of block until the wall is about 18" above ground level, staggering the vertical joints.

Fill behind the wall with crushed stone and pack it thoroughly with the hand tamper. Lay the remaining courses of block, except for the cap row. Backfill with crushed stone and pack with the tamper as you go.

Before laying the cap block, fold the end of the landscape fabric over the crushed stone backfill. Add a layer of topsoil over the fabric, and then pack it thoroughly with a hand tamper. Trim off any excess landscape fabric.

Apply construction adhesive to the top course of block, then lay the cap block. Follow the stone manufacturer's instructions for adhesive use. Use topsoil to fill in behind the wall and to fill in the base at the front of the wall. Install sod or plants, as desired.

How to Add a Curve to an Interlocking Block Retaining Wall

Outline the curve by first driving a stake at each end and then driving another stake at the point where lines extended from the first stakes would form a right angle. Tie a mason's string to the right-angle stake, extended to match the distance to the other two stakes, establishing the radius of the curve. Mark the curve by swinging flour or spray paint at the string end, like a compass.

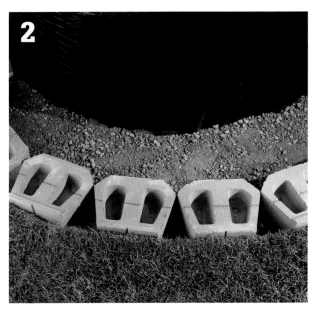

Excavate for the wall section, following the curved layout line. To install the first course of landscape blocks, turn them upside down and backwards and align them with the radius curve. Use a level to ensure the blocks sit level and are properly placed.

Install subsequent courses so the overlapping flange sits flush against the back of the blocks in the course below. As you install each course, the radius will change because of the backwards pitch of the wall, affecting the layout of the courses. Where necessary, trim blocks to size. Install using landscape construction adhesive, taking care to maintain the running-bond pattern.

Use half blocks or cut blocks to create finished ends on open ends of the wall.

These convenient interlocking pavers are made with DIYers in mind. They are easy to install and often come with fully plotted patterns for simple design preparation and installation.

Cobblestone Paver Patio

Concrete pavers have advanced by leaps and bounds from the monochromatic, cookie-cutter bricks and slabs associated with first-generation versions. The latest products feature subtle color blends that lend themselves well to organic, irregular patterns. A tumbling process during manufacturing can further "age" the pavers so they look more like natural cobblestones. The technological advances in the casting and finishing processes have become so sophisticated that a well-selected concrete paver patio could look as suitable in a traditional European square as in a suburban back yard.

When choosing pavers for a patio, pick a style and blend of shapes and sizes that complements your landscape. Use the materials used on your house's exterior and other stone or masonry in your yard to inform your decisions on colors and shade. Be aware that some paver styles require set purchase amounts, and it's not always possible to return partially used pallets of material, so order carefully.

In this project, we lay a cobblestone patio that uses three sizes of pavers (see page 58). Such pavers may be purchased by a fraction of a pallet, or band, minimizing leftovers. We've also included a row of edge pavers to create a pleasing border around the patio. When shopping for your own patio materials, bring a drawing of your patio plans with exact measurements to your stone yard or landscape supplier. Based on your chosen pattern, the sales staff will be able to tell you how much stone in each size you'll need to purchase.

The patio in this project was created using the following sizes and proportions of cobblestone concrete pavers:

Field pavers—70 percent 6 × 9" cobble rectangles, 30 percent 6 × 6" cobble squares

Border pavers—3 × 6" cobble rectangles

Tools & Materials ▸

Excavation tools	Masonry saw
Wheelbarrow	Push broom
4-ft. level	Concrete pavers
Hand maul	Compactable gravel
Wood stakes	Coarse sand
Chalk line	Plastic edging and
Mason's string	spikes
Line level	Joint sand
Square-nose spade	Eye and ear
1"-dia. metal pipes	protection
2 × 4 lumber	Work gloves
Scrap plywood	Tape measure
Plate compactor	Shovel

Cobblestones ▸

Today, the word "cobblestone" more often refers to cast concrete masonry units that mimic the look of natural cobblestones. Although they are tumbled to give them a slightly aged appearance, cast concrete cobbles are more uniform in shape, size, and color. This is an advantage when it comes to installation, but purists object to the appearance.

Cobblestone Paver Patio—Construction Details

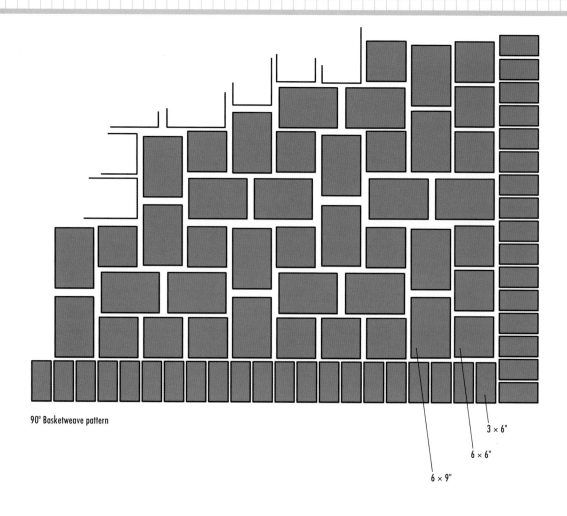

90° Basketweave pattern

3 × 6"

6 × 6"

6 × 9"

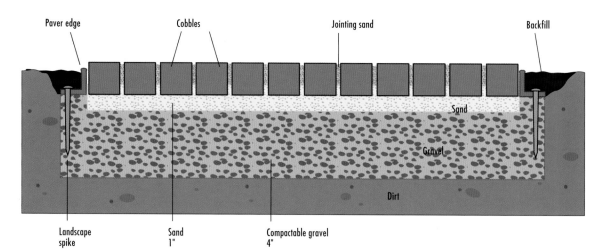

Paver edge

Cobbles

Jointing sand

Backfill

Sand

Gravel

Dirt

Landscape
spike

Sand
1"

Compactable gravel
4"

How to Build a Cobblestone Paver Patio

Mark the corners of the finished patio with stakes, and remove any sod or other plantings in the area. Set up grade stakes and mason's strings to guide the excavation and establish a downward slope of 1/8" per foot away from the house foundation.

Variation: Use batterboards and mason's strings to establish the layout of the project area. See pages 40 to 45 for detailed instructions.

Excavate the site to a depth that accommodates a 4" gravel subbase, a 1" layer of sand, and the thickness of the pavers (minus the desired height above the ground). Extend the excavation 6" beyond the patio footprint. Use the layout strings or grade stakes to check the depth and slope as you work. Tamp the soil with a plate compactor.

Add compactable gravel for a 4"-thick layer after compaction. Screed the gravel flat with a straight 2 × 4 and use a level or the layout strings to make sure the surface is properly sloped. Compact the gravel thoroughly with a plate compactor.

(continued)

Set up a new string layout to guide the edging installation using stakes and mason's string. The strings should represent the inside edges of the edging material. To make sure the layout has square corners, measure diagonally between the corners: the layout is square when the measurements are equal. See pages 40 to 45.

Install rigid paver edging along one side edge of the patio: snap a chalk line directly under the layout string along the edge, and then remove that string. Set the edging to the line and secure it with paver edge spikes, driving in the spikes only partially (in case you have to make adjustments later).

Screed (2 × 4)

Screed guides
(1" pipe)

Lay lengths of 1"-dia. metal pipe in the project area to serve as screed guides. Fill the patio area with coarse building sand to the tops of the pipes. Screed the sand smooth and flat using a long, straight 2 × 4, pulling the board back and forth with a sawing motion. Remove the pipes, fill the voids with sand, and smooth the surface flat. *Tip: Dampen the sand before screeding.*

7

Edging
90° corner

Bond line

Set the pavers in the chosen pattern, starting at the 90° corner formed by the patio edging and an adjacent layout string (called the bond line). Lay border pavers along one or both edges before setting the field pavers. For now, simply lay the pavers in place; later, you will bed them into the sand with the plate vibrator.

Bond line

Perpendicular to bond line

A

B

Strings A and B are equal in length to create right angles.

Option: Use additional layout strings to help guide the paver pattern. Set up a string that is perpendicular to the bond line, using it to align courses every few feet. Tie equidistant strings between the corners and the end of the perpendicular string to assure a right angle with the bond line.

8

Paver edging

Install the remaining pieces of edging as you near the opposite side and end of the patio, leaving enough room for the final course of field pavers (plus border units, if applicable). Cut away the edges of the sand bed so the edging rests on the gravel base only. *Tip: If you don't need to cut pavers along the edges, you can install the edging after all of the pavers are laid.*

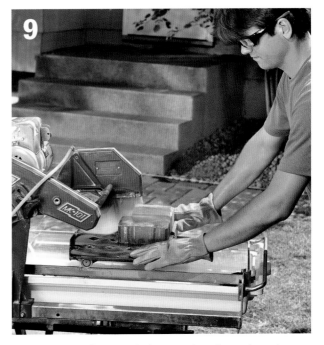

9

Cut pavers to fit as needed to complete the paving using a rented masonry saw (also see Making Curves on page 62). It's preferable to cut pavers a little too small than to have very tight fits; the joint sand will fill small gaps. With the paving complete, drive the edging stakes into the rigid edging to lock the pavers in place.

(continued)

10

Sweep joint sand over the pavers using a push broom. Continue adding sand and sweeping until the joints between pavers are nearly filled to the top surface.

11

Tamp the patio surface with the plate compactor. Move the compactor in circular motions, working from the outside in and overlapping rings as you go. Repeat Steps 10 and 11 until the joints are completely filled after compaction. *Note: Some paver manufacturers recommend sweeping excess sand from the pavers before compacting.*

Making Curves ▸

At rounded corners and curves, install border pavers (A) in a fan pattern with even gaps between the pavers. Gentle curves may accommodate full-sized border pavers, but for sharper turns you usually need to cut tapers into the paver edges so you don't end up with wide gaps at the outside. When using border pavers in a curved layout, the field pavers will need to be trimmed to fit the odd spaces created where the field and borders intersect (B).

Choosing Pavers & Patterns ▸

The number of purchasing options available when you shop for pavers makes it possible to create just about any patio layout pattern you can imagine. There is nothing stopping you from going wild and creating a layout that's truly one-of-a-kind. Most landscape centers will also work with you to create a layout for your patio that employs tested design ideas and uses pavers in a very efficient manner and with as little cutting as possible.

Another option for DIY designers is to visit the website of the paver manufacturer (you should be able to get the information from your paver dealer). Many of these have applications where you can choose a basic style you like (such as the patterns shown here) and enter the size of your planned patio. You'll receive a printout of what the pattern should look like, along with a shopping list for the materials you'll need, all the way down to sand and spikes for your paver edging.

A traditional brick running-bond pattern can be created using rectangular pavers.

This basketweave pattern is made with squares and large rectangles. A border of small rectangles completes the design.

Cobblestone paving with squares and large and small rectangles create this circular pattern.

Circular Paver Patio

Tools & Materials ▸

Circular saw	Marking paint
Hammer	2½" drywall screws
Drill	Compactable gravel
Excavation tools	Landscape fabric
Mason's string	1 or 1½" pipe
Line level	Straight 2 × 4
Plate compactor	Washed concrete
Trowel	sand
Flathead screwdriver	Scrap plywood
Shovel	Plastic patio edging
Push broom	Paver joint sand
Circular paver units	Eye and ear
16d nails	protection
Duct tape	Work gloves
Lumber (2 × 2, 2 × 4)	Tape measure

Concrete pavers are available in a range of sizes and shapes, making it easy to create distinctive patterns without a lot of cuts. This circular patio is made with a complete set of shaped concrete pavers. To create a perfect circle, all you have to do is set the pavers following the manufacturer's installation diagram, and no cuts are needed (although some sets have center pieces that must be cut before installation).

Circular paver sets are commonly sold in fixed starter sizes, and you can add units as needed to enlarge the circle. You may have to purchase additional pavers as complete sets or in full-pallet quantities and use only what you need. Circular pavers are ideal for building freestanding patios because their shape makes for a nice decorative feature.

A circular patio is visually dynamic and its shape makes it uniquely suited to intimate outdoor dining and entertaining spaces. When shopping for pavers, ask about color and texture options. Some suppliers may allow you to mix and match finishes for a personalized look.

As a design feature, a circle naturally draws the eye toward its center. This makes a circular patio the perfect setting for a round patio table and chairs or for highlighting a central decorative feature, such as a fountain or statuary. A circle is also the best configuration for creating an intimate seating area surrounding a fire pit. In addition to patio spaces, small circles can be used as landing areas along a curving paver walkway, while an open ring of circular pavers can be used as a border around a planting bed.

The patio in this project follows a standard sandset installation. Mortaring a patio like this would be far more difficult than sandsetting, due to the irregularity of the paver joints. For the sandset process, it's easiest to lay the pavers first, and then install flexible plastic edging around the perimeter to lock the units in place. If your patio plan calls for numerous cuts, rent a masonry saw, or *tub saw*, for making the cuts. Otherwise, you can make a few cuts with a circular saw fitted with a masonry blade. Before you get started, it will help to review the detailed information on laying out the project site and preparing the gravel base (see pages 40 to 45).

Circular Paver Materials ▸

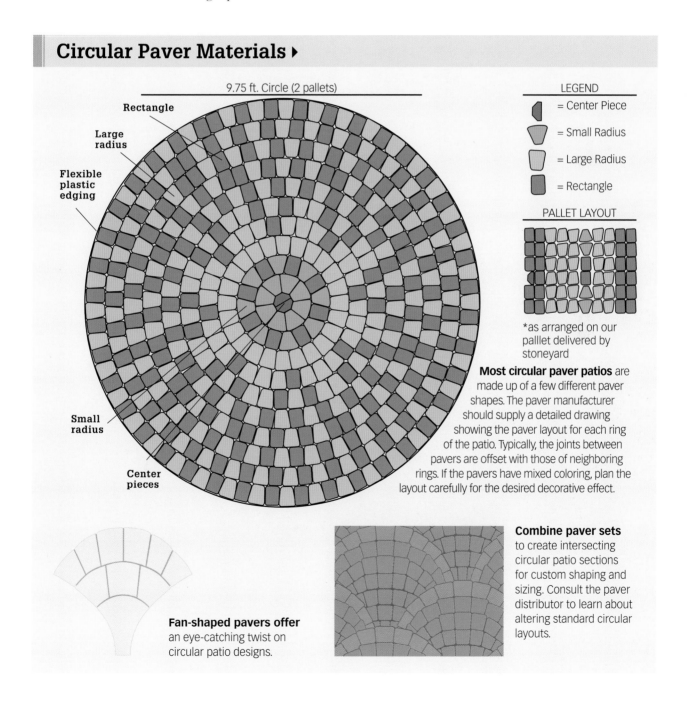

9.75 ft. Circle (2 pallets)

Rectangle

Large radius

Flexible plastic edging

Small radius

Center pieces

LEGEND

= Center Piece

= Small Radius

= Large Radius

= Rectangle

PALLET LAYOUT

*as arranged on our palllet delivered by stoneyard

Most circular paver patios are made up of a few different paver shapes. The paver manufacturer should supply a detailed drawing showing the paver layout for each ring of the patio. Typically, the joints between pavers are offset with those of neighboring rings. If the pavers have mixed coloring, plan the layout carefully for the desired decorative effect.

Fan-shaped pavers offer an eye-catching twist on circular patio designs.

Combine paver sets to create intersecting circular patio sections for custom shaping and sizing. Consult the paver distributor to learn about altering standard circular layouts.

How to Install a Circular Paver Patio

Create a center pivot for defining the patio layout. Drive a stake at the exact center of the desired location for the finished patio. Cut a straight 2 × 2 about 12" longer than the radius of the patio. Drill a large pilot hole at one end of the board, and fasten the board to the center of the stake with a single nail. *Note: For large patio areas, use a string tied to a center nail instead of a board (inset).*

Mark the ground for excavation. Measuring out from the nail, mark the board at a distance equal to the radius, plus 6". Tape a can of marking paint to the board so the spray nozzle is centered on the mark (inset). Spray a continuous line onto the ground while pivoting the board to create a complete circle. Set up batterboards and leveled layout strings in a square that's about 1 ft. larger than the excavated area. Remove all sod and other vegetation inside the marked circle.

Measure diagonally between opposing corners and adjust the strings as needed until the measurements are equal (the layout is square). Slope two of the parallel layout strings at ¼" per foot using the distance between the batterboards to calculate the drop distance generally dropping away from your house.

Excavate the site to the depth recommended by the paver manufacturer. Make sure the soil is smooth, well compacted, and properly sloped to ⅛" per foot.

Prepare the subbase with a 4" layer of gravel. Thoroughly compact the gravel with a plate compactor.

Check the depth with cross strings and a story pole as you work (shown). The completed base must be smooth and flat and follow the slope setting.

Install landscape fabric over the gravel subbase. Overlap the edges of fabric strips by 6". Trim the fabric as needed, leaving the ends a little long for now. *Note: This helps keep the sand base in place longer.*

Set two lengths of 1"-dia. pipe on top of the landscape fabric so that one piece spans the full diameter of the gravel base and the other spans across the base about ¼ of the way in from the side of the circle. Align the pipes parallel to each other. Fill half of the patio site with sand even with the tops of the pipes.

Use a straight 2 × 4 to screed the sand level with the pipes. Move the short pipe to the opposite side of the site to complete the other half of the sand layer. Remove the pipes and then fill all depressions with sand. *Tip: Moisten sand prior to screeding.*

(continued)

Position the center paver, then measure out to the edge of the site in several places to confirm that it is centered. *Tip: Work on top of a piece of plywood to avoid disturbing the sand bed.*

Set the first ring of pavers around the center paver. Check their positions carefully, and make sure the spacing lugs are oriented correctly. If the pavers don't have lugs, gap them according to the manufacturer's specifications. *Note: Do not hammer or tamp the pavers into the sand bed unless the manufacturer directs otherwise.*

Set the remaining pavers, completing each ring according to your layout diagram. Be sure to offset the paver joints between rows. The pavers may be labeled, requiring them to be installed in a specific order as you work around the circle. After a sizable area is laid, work from your plywood platform set atop the pavers.

Install rigid paver edging along the patio's perimeter. Set the edging on top of the gravel subbase but not the sand bed. *Tip: Dampening the sand bed along the patio edge makes it easy to cut the sand away cleanly with a trowel before setting the edging.*

Inspect the paving to make sure all joints are aligned properly and all gaps are consistent. Make minor adjustments to pavers as needed using a flathead screwdriver as a pry bar. Be careful not to mar the paver edges as you pry.

Shovel joint sand over the entire patio surface, then use a push broom to sweep the sand over the pavers to fill the joints. Repeat as needed until the joints are completely filled, then sweep off excess sand.

Set the pavers into the sand bed using a plate compactor. Make a first pass along the perimeter of the patio, then compact the interior with parallel back-and-forth passes, overlapping the preceding pass slightly as you go. *Note: Avoid excessive tamping to prevent damage to the paver surfaces.* Add another application of sand. Tamp the surface, but make the interior passes perpendicular to those of the first tamping runs.

Refill the joints with sand a final time and sweep the surface clean. Spray thoroughly with water to settle the joint sand.

Mortared Paver Patio

Setting brick or concrete pavers into mortar is one of the most beautiful—and permanent—ways to dress up an old concrete slab patio. The paving style used most often for mortared pavers is the standard running bond pattern, that is also the easiest pattern to install.

Mortared pavers are appropriate for old concrete slabs that are flat, structurally sound, and relatively free of cracks. Minor surface flaws are generally acceptable, however existing slabs with significant cracks or any evidence of shifting or other structural problems will most likely pass on those same flaws to the paver finish. When in doubt, have your slab assessed by a qualified mason or concrete contractor to learn about your options.

Pavers for mortaring include natural clay brick units in both standard thickness (2⅜") and thinner versions (1½") and concrete pavers in various shapes and sizes. Any type you choose should be square-edged, to simplify the application and finishing of the mortar joints. When shopping for pavers, discuss your project with an expert masonry supplier. Areas that experience harsh winters call for the hardiest pavers available, graded SW or SX for severe weather. Also make sure the mortar you use is compatible with the pavers to minimize the risk of cracking and other problems.

Tools & Materials ▸

Stiff brush or broom	⅜ or ½" plywood
Rented masonry saw	Spray bottle
Mason's trowel	Isolation board
Mortar mixing tools	Mortar
4-ft. level	Burlap
Rubber mallet	Plastic sheeting
Mortar bag	Notched board
Jointing tool	Mason's string
Pointing trowel	Straight 2 × 4
Concrete cleaner or	Eye and ear
pressure washer	protection
Brick or concrete	Push broom
pavers	Work gloves

Nothing dresses up an old concrete patio like mortared pavers. The mortaring process takes more time and effort than many finishing techniques, but the look is timeless; and the surface is extremely durable.

How to Install a Mortared Paver Patio

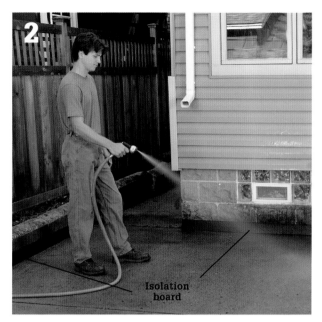

Prepare the patio surface for mortar by thoroughly cleaning the concrete with a commercial concrete cleaner and/or a pressure washer. Make sure the surface is completely free of dirt, grease, oil, and waxy residue.

Mist the concrete with water to prevent premature drying of the mortar bed, and then mix a batch of mortar as directed by the manufacturer. *Tip: Install isolation board along the foundation wall if the paving abuts the house; this prevents the mortar from bonding with the foundation.*

Dry-lay the border pavers along the edge of the patio slab. Gap the pavers to simulate the mortar joints using spacers cut from plywood equal to the joint thickness (⅜ or ½" is typical). Adjust the pavers as needed to create a pleasing layout with the fewest cuts possible. Mark the paver locations on the slab and then set pavers aside.

Begin laying the border pavers by spreading a ½"-thick layer of mortar for three or four pavers along one edge of the patio using a mason's trowel. Lay the first few pavers, buttering the leading edge of each with enough mortar to create the desired joint thickness. Press or tap each paver in place to slightly compress the mortar bed. If necessary, cut bricks with a rented masonry saw.

(continued)

5

Remove excess mortar from the tops and sides of the pavers. Use a level to make sure the pavers are even across the tops, and check the mortar joints for uniform thickness. Tool the joints with a jointer as you go. Repeat the process to lay the remaining border pavers. Allow mortar to dry.

Option: To conceal the edges of a raised slab, build wood forms similar to concrete forms (see page 153). Set a gap between the forms and slab equal to the paver thickness plus ½".

6

Dry lay the field pavers without buttering them. Use the plywood spacers to set the gaps for mortar joints. Cut end pavers as needed with a rented masonry saw. *Tip: Keep the courses straight by setting the pavers along a string line referenced from the border pavers. Remove dry-laid pavers.*

7

Spacer

Notched screed

Spread and then screed mortar for the field pavers. Trowel on a ½"-thick layer of mortar inside the border, covering only about 3 or 4 sq. ft. to allow for working time before the mortar sets. Screed the mortar to a uniform ½" thickness using a notched board set atop the border pavers (set the interior end on a lumber spacer, as needed).

8

As you work, check the heights of the pavers with a level or a straight 2 × 4 to make sure all units are level with one another. If a paver is too high, press it down or tap it with a rubber mallet; if too low, lift it out and butter its back face with mortar and reset it. Repeat steps 6 through 8 to complete the paver installation, and then let the mortar bed dry.

9

Fill the paver joints with fresh mortar using a mortar bag to keep the paver faces clean. Within each working section, fill the long joints between courses first, and then do the short joints between the paver ends. Overfill the joints slightly.

10

Tool the joints with a jointing tool—again, complete the long joints first and then fill the next section. As the mortar begins to set (turns from glossy wet to flat gray) in each tooled section, scrape off excess mortar with a pointing trowel, being careful not to smear mortar onto the pavers.

11

Let the mortar joints dry for a few hours, and then scrub the pavers with a wet burlap rag to remove excess mortar and any other residue. Cover the surface with plastic for 48 hours. Remove the plastic, and let the surface cure undisturbed for one week before using the patio.

Sandset flagstone patios blend nicely with natural landscapes. Although flagstone evokes a natural feel, the patio can appear rustic or formal. This patio has clean, well-tamped joints and straight, groomed edges along the perimeter that lends to a formal feel. Plantings in the joints or a rough, natural perimeter would give the same patio a more relaxed, rustic feel.

Sandset Flagstone Patio

Flagstones make a great, long-lasting patio surface with a naturally rough texture and a perfectly imperfect look and finish. Randomly shaped stones are especially suited to patios with curved borders, but they can also be cut to form straight lines. Your patio will appear more at home in your landscape if the flagstones you choose are of the same stone species as other stones in the area. For example, if your gravel paths and walls are made from a local buff limestone, look for the same material in limestone flags.

Flagstones usually come in large slabs, sold as flagstone, or in smaller pieces (typically 16" or smaller), sold as *steppers*. You can make a patio out of either. Larger stones will make a solid patio with a more even surface, but the bigger ones can require three strong people to position, and large stones are hard to cut and fit tightly. If your soil drains well and is stable, flagstones can be laid on nothing more than a layer of sand. However, if you have unstable clay soil that becomes soft when wet, start with a 4"-thick foundation of compactable gravel (see pages 40 to 45) under your sand.

There are a few different options for filling the spaces between flagstones. One popular treatment is to plant them with low-growing perennials suited to crevice culture. For best results, use sand-based soil between flagstones when planting. Also, stick to very small plants that can withstand foot traffic. If you prefer not to have a planted patio, simply fill the joints with sand or fine gravel—just be sure to add landscape fabric under your sand base to discourage weed growth.

The following project includes steps for building a classic flagstone patio. You'll also find instructions for building low dry stone walls, the ultimate add-on to a stone patio surface. If you're new to working with natural stone, see pages 82 to 83 for some basic cutting tips.

Tools & Materials ▸

Mason's string	Stiff-bristle brush
Line level	Circular saw with
Rope or hose	masonry blade
Excavation tools	Plugs or seeds for
Spud bar	groundcover
Broom	Eye and ear
Stakes	protection
Marking paint	Work gloves
1" (outside	¾" plywood
diameter) pipe	3½" deck screws
Coarse sand	Pointing chisel
Straight 2 × 4	Pitching chisel
Flagstone	Stone chisel
Spray bottle	Hand maul
Stone edging	Dust mask
Sand-based soil or	Chalk or a crayon
joint sand	Square-nose spade
Lumber (2 × 2,	Crushed stone
2 × 4)	Ashlar
Drill	Mortar
Mason's trowel	Capstones

Adding a Stone Wall ▸

A dry stone wall is a simple, beautiful addition to a flagstone patio. A wall functions as extra seating, a place to set plants, or extra countertop or tabletop space. It also provides visual definition to your outdoor space. See page 80 for how to build a stone wall.

Construction Details

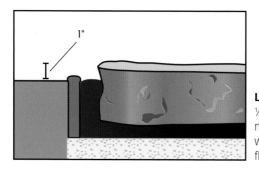

Lay flagstones so their tops are approximately ½ to 1" above the surrounding ground. Because natural stones are not uniform in thickness, you will need to adjust sand or dirt beneath each flagstone, as needed.

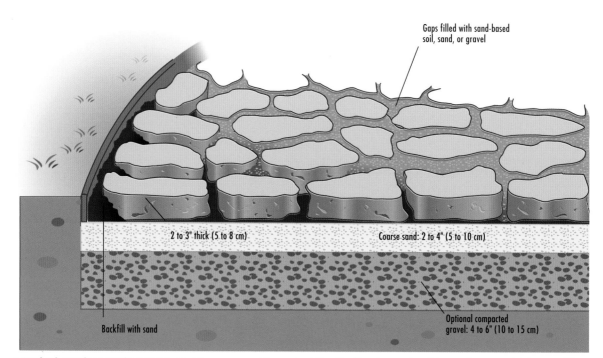

Gaps filled with sand-based soil, sand, or gravel

2 to 3" thick (5 to 8 cm)

Coarse sand: 2 to 4" (5 to 10 cm)

Backfill with sand

Optional compacted gravel: 4 to 6" (10 to 15 cm)

A typical sandset patio has a layer of coarse sand for embedding the flagstones. A subbase of compactable gravel is an option for improved stability and drainage. The joints between stones can be filled with sand, gravel, or soil and plants. Edging material is optional.

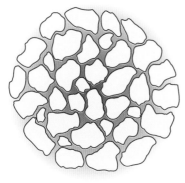

Irregular flagstones look natural and are easy to work with in round layouts.

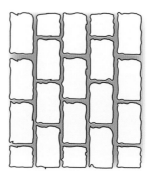

Flagstones that are cut into rectangular shapes can be laid in square or rectangular patterns with uniform gaps.

How to Build a Sandset Flagstone Patio

1

Outline the patio base using string and stakes for straight lines and/or a rope or hose for curves. The base should extend at least 2 to 4" beyond the edges of the flagstones, except where the patio will butt up to a wall. Transfer the outline to the ground with marking paint. Remove any sod and vegetation within the base area.

2

Set up layout strings to guide the excavation using stakes or batterboards (see pages 40 to 45 for detailed steps on layout and site preparation). Excavate the base to a depth of 2" + the stone thickness plus ½ to 1". Slope the ground away from the house foundation at a rate of ¼" per foot.

3

Lay sections of 1" pipe across the project area to serve as screed gauges. These allow you to strike off sand at a consistent depth when you drag a screed board over them. *Note: Since large flagstones can be held in place adequately by the surrounding soil, edging for the patio is optional; it often looks best to allow neighboring groundcover to grow up to the edges of the stones. If you do plan to use edging, install it now.*

4

Screed

Gauges

Fill the site with coarse sand slightly above the screed gauges. With a helper, drag a straight 2 × 4 across the screed gauges to level off the sand. Use a screed board that's long enough so that you can avoid stepping in the sand. Work the screed in a back-and-forth sawing motion. Remove the pipes once each section is finished, fill in the voids and smooth the surface flat.

(continued)

Arrange your flagstones into groups according to size and shape. As a general rule, start paving with the broadest stones and fill in around them with increasingly smaller pieces, but appearance and sight lines are also important: if there is one nice stone with a flat surface and good color, feature it in the center of the patio. Or, if some of the patio will be visible from the house, choose nicer stones for these areas.

Begin by laying large, thick stones around the perimeter of the patio. Leave a consistent gap of about 1" between stones by matching pieces like a puzzle and cutting and dressing stones as needed (see pages 82 to 83). The outer edge of the patio should form smooth curves (or straight lines) without jutting pieces or abrupt irregularities. Level stones as needed by prying up with a spud bar and adding or removing sand underneath.

Fill in around the larger stones with smaller pieces cut to fit the spaces, as needed, working from the outside in. After setting a band of stones a few courses wide, lay a 2 × 4 across the stones to make sure they're level with one another. Add or remove sand below to adjust their height, and dampen the sand occasionally to make it easier to work with.

Fill the joints between stones with sand-based, weed-seed-free soil (see page 79). Sweep the soil across the patio surface to fill the cracks, and then water the soil so it settles. Repeat as needed until the soil reaches the desired level. Plant plugs or seeds for groundcover to grow up between the stones, if desired.

Variation: To finish the patio with sand instead of soil and plants, spread sand over the patio and sweep across the stones with a push broom to fill the joints. Pack the sand with your fingers or a piece of wood. Spray the entire area with water to help compact the sand. Let the patio dry. Repeat filling and spraying until the joints are full and the stones are securely locked in place.

Choosing Soil & Plants for Your Patio ▸

Sand-based soil (also called "patio planting" soil) is the best material to use for planting between flagstones. This mixture of soil and sand sweeps easily into joints, and it resists tight compaction to promote healthy plant growth, as well as surface drainage. Regular soil can become too compacted for effective planting and drainage and soil from your yard will undoubtedly contain weeds. Sand-based soil is available in bulk or by the bag and is often custom-mixed at most large garden centers.

As for the best plants to use, listed below are a few species that tend to do well in a patio application. Ask a local supplier what works best for your climate.

Patio "planting soil" (for planting between stones) is available in bulk or bags at most garden centers. It is good for filling cracks because the sand base makes it dry and smooth enough to sweep into cracks, yet the black compost will support plant growth. Because it is bagged, you can be assured it doesn't come with weeds.

- Alyssum
- Rock cress
- Thrift
- Miniature dianthus
- Candytuft
- Lobelia
- Forget-me-not
- Saxifrage
- Sedum
- Thymus
- Scotch moss
- Irish moss
- Woolly thyme
- Mock strawberry

Building a Dry Stone Patio Wall

Stone walls are beautiful, long-lasting structures that are surprisingly easy to build, provided you plan carefully. A low stone wall can be constructed without mortar, using a centuries-old method known as dry laying. With this technique, the wall is actually formed by two separate stacks that lean together slightly. The position and weight of the two stacks support each other, forming a single, sturdy wall. A dry stone wall can be built to any length, but its width must be at least half of its height.

You can purchase stone for this project from a quarry or stone supplier, where different sizes, shapes, and colors of stone are sold, priced by the ton. The quarry or stone center can also sell you type M mortar—necessary for bonding the capstones to the top of the wall.

Building dry stone walls requires patience and a fair amount of physical effort. The stones must be sorted by size and shape. You'll probably also need to shape some of the stones to achieve consistent spacing and a general appearance that appeals to you.

It's easiest to build a dry stone wall with ashlar—stone that has been split into roughly rectangular blocks. Ashlar stone is stacked in the same running bond pattern used in brick wall construction; each stone overlaps a joint in the underlying course. This technique prevents long vertical joints, that weaken the structure and detract from its appearance.

A low dry stone wall is the perfect complement for a flagstone patio. Walls can enclose one or more sides of the patio or even provide seating along the perimeter. For comfortable seating, build your wall 16 to 18" tall and top it with smooth capstones for a flat, clean finish. In most cases, it's easiest to build walls before laying the patio surface.

How to Build a Dry Stone Wall

Lay out the wall site, using stakes and mason's string. Dig a 6"-deep trench that extends 6" beyond the wall on all sides. Add a 4" crushed stone subbase to the trench, creating a "V" shape by sloping the subbase so the center is about 2" deeper than the edges.

Select appropriate stones and lay the first course. Place pairs of stones side by side, flush with the edges of the trench and sloping toward the center. Use stones of similar height; position uneven sides face down. Fill any gaps between the shaping stones with small filler stones.

Lay the next course, staggering the joints. Use pairs of stones of varying lengths to offset the center joint. Alternate stone length, and keep the height even, stacking pairs of thin stones if necessary to maintain consistent height. Place filler stones in the gaps.

Filler stones

Every other course, place a tie stone every 3 ft. You may need to split the tie stones to length. Check the wall periodically for level.

Tie stones

Mortar the capstones to the top of the wall, keeping the mortar at least 6" from the edges so it's not visible. Push the capstones together and mortar the cracks in between. Brush off dried excess mortar with a stiff-bristle brush. Add patio, if desired (see page 75).

Cutting Stone ▸

You can cut most stone by placing it directly on a bed of flat, soft ground, such as grass or sand, that will absorb some of the shock when the maul strikes the chisel. If you plan to do a lot of cutting or splitting, construct a banker, a simple sand-bed table that provides a sturdy, shock-absorbent work surface (shown at right).

For basic cuts and cleaning up stone faces (called dressing), the best tools are a pointing chisel, a pitching chisel, a basic stone chisel, and a hand maul. A circular saw also comes in handy for when you need a very straight edge or to help reduce the work of scoring many stones with a chisel. Always wear eye protection when cutting or dressing stone.

To build a banker for cutting stone, construct two square frames out of 2 × 2s, and sandwich a matching piece of ¾" plywood between the frames. Fasten the pieces together with 3½" deck screws driven through both sides. Fill one side of the banker with sand to complete the work surface.

Cutting Stone with a Circular Saw

A circular saw lets you precut stones with broad surfaces with greater control and accuracy than most people can achieve with a chisel. It's a noisy tool, so wear earplugs, along with a dust mask and safety goggles. Install a toothless masonry blade on your saw and start out with the blade set to cut ⅛" deep. (Make sure the blade is designed for the material you're cutting. Some masonry blades are designed for hard materials like concrete, marble, and granite. Others are for soft materials, like concrete block, brick, flagstone, and limestone.) Wet the stone before cutting to help control dust, then make three passes, setting the blade ⅛" deeper with each pass. Repeat the process on the other side. A thin piece of wood under the saw protects the saw foot from rough masonry surfaces. Remember: always use a GFCI outlet or extension cord when using power tools outdoors.

How to Cut Flagstone

Mark the stone for cutting on both sides using chalk or a crayon. If there is a fissure nearby, mark your line there, since the stone will likely break there naturally. *Note: To prevent unpredicted breaks when cutting off large pieces, plan to chip off small sections at a time.*

Score along the cut line on the backside of the stone (the side that won't be exposed) by moving a stone chisel along the line and striking it with moderate blows with a maul. As an alternative, you can do this step with a circular saw.

Break the stone to complete the cut: first, turn the stone over and rest it on a metal pipe or a 2 × 4 so the scored edge is directly over the support. Then, strike forcefully near the end of the waste portion to break the stone along the cut line.

Dressing Stones for Walls

Laying stones works best when the sides (including the top and bottom) are roughly square. If a side is sharply skewed, score and split it with a pitching chisel, and chip off smaller peaks with a pointing chisel or mason's hammer. Remember: a stone should sit flat on its bottom or top side without much rocking.

"Dress" a stone using a pointing chisel and maul to remove jagged edges or undesirable bumps. Position the chisel at a 30 to 45° angle at the base of the piece to be removed. Tap lightly all around the break line, then more forcefully, to chip off the piece. Position the chisel carefully before each blow with the maul.

Mortared Flagstone Patio

With its permanent, solid finish, mortared flagstone provides a more formal patio setting than sandset stone. It also has a cleaner feel, because there's no sand to get kicked up out of the joints. Yet the mortared application offers the same organic appeal and dramatic lines of any natural flagstone surface. You can achieve an even more formal look with cut flagstone installed in a grid layout.

The proper base for mortaring flagstone is a structurally sound concrete slab. If you're covering an old concrete patio, inspect the slab for signs of structural problems. Wide cracks and uneven surfaces indicate shifting soil or an insufficient subbase. This movement most likely will continue, leading to cracks in your new stone surface. You should remove the old slab and pour a new one or consider sand-setting the stone over the slab.

One of the nice things about mortaring stone over concrete is that you don't need edging to contain the stones. This gives you the option of leaving the edges rough to enhance the natural look, or you can hang the outer stones over the edges of the slab to conceal the concrete below.

Tools & Materials ▸

Paint roller
Stone chisel
Maul
Circular saw with
  masonry blade
Mortar box or
  wheelbarrow
Masonry hoe
Mason's trowel
Concrete float
Rubber mallet
4-ft. level
Straight 2 × 4
Grout bag
Stiff-bristle brush
Sponge or coarse rag
Jointing tool
Whiskbroom
Concrete bonding
  agent
Mortar
Flagstone
Stone sealer
  (optional)
Eye and ear
  protection
Work gloves
Concrete cleaning
  supplies
Chalk
Tape measure
Acrylic fortifier
Loose gravel and
  small rocks

The flagstone patio is a classic element of modern landscape design. Bluestone (above) is one of the most popular types, but may not be available in all areas since specific types vary by region.

How to Build a Mortared Flagstone Patio

Thoroughly clean the concrete slab. While the slab doesn't need to be in perfect condition, it does need to be sound. Repair large cracks or holes. After repairs have cured, apply a latex bonding agent to the patio surface, following the manufacturer's instructions.

Once the bonding agent has set up per the manufacturer's recommendations, dry-lay stones on the patio to determine an appealing layout. Work from the center outward and evenly distribute large stones and smaller ones, with ½ to 1" joints between them.

Cut stones to size as needed: mark the cutting lines with chalk, then cut the stones with a stone chisel (or circular saw) and maul (see pages 82 to 83 for tips on cutting stone).

Variation: For a more rustic appearance, allow stones to overhang the edges of the slab. Stones thicker in size can overhang as much as 6", provided that the slab supports at least two-thirds of the stone. Thinner stones should not overhang more than 3". After stones are mortared in place, fill in beneath the overhanging stones with soil.

(continued)

Mix a stiff batch of Type N or S mortar, following the manufacturer's directions. Starting near the center of the patio, set aside some of the stone, maintaining the layout pattern. Spread a 2"-thick layer of mortar onto the slab using a concrete float.

Firmly press the first large stone into the mortar, in its same position as in the layout. Tap the stone with a rubber mallet or the handle of the trowel to set it. Use a 4-ft. level and a scrap 2 × 4 to check for level; make any necessary adjustments.

Using the first stone as a reference for the course height, continue to lay stones in mortar, working from the center of the slab to the edges. Maintain ½ to 1" joints.

Check for level often as you work, using a straight length of 2 × 4 and the 4-ft. level. Tap stones to make minor adjustments. Once you're done, let the mortar set up for a day or two before walking on it or grouting.

Use a grout bag to fill the joints with mortar (add acrylic fortifier to the mix to make the mortar more elastic). Do not overfill the joints. Pack loose gravel and small rocks into gaps first to conserve mortar and make stronger joints. Wipe up spilled mortar.

Once the mortar is stiff enough that your thumb leaves an impression without mortar sticking to it, rake the joints just enough so the mortar is even with the surface of the stone, so water cannot pool. Use a whisk broom to shape the mortar.

Allow the mortar to cure for a few days, then clean the patio with water and a stiff-bristle brush. After the mortar cures for a week, apply a stone sealer, following the manufacturer's instructions.

The moldable nature of poured concrete makes it ideal for creating patios with curves and custom shapes in addition to perfect squares and rectangles. If your patio plans call for a neighboring concrete walkway, see pages 150 to 155.

Concrete Slab Patio

Few outdoor surfaces are as heavy-duty as a properly poured concrete slab. As a patio material, poured concrete is tough to beat. The surface is flat, smooth, easy to clean, and about as close to maintenance-free as you can get. A concrete slab is also the best foundation for permanent finishes like mortared brick, tile, and stone. And if you like the simplicity and durability of a bare concrete patio but flat gray doesn't suit your design scheme, you can always apply an acid stain, dry pigment colors, or concrete paint (rated for exterior use) for custom coloring effects without compromising the surface's performance.

If you've never worked with poured concrete before, you'll find that most of the work lies in preparing the site and building the forms for containing and shaping the wet concrete. Once the concrete is mixed or delivered to your site, time is of the essence, and the best way to ensure quality results is to be prepared with strong forms, the right tools, and an understanding of each step of the process. And it never hurts to have help: you'll need at least two hardworking assistants for the placing and finishing stages. See pages 98 to 99 for some more useful information on working with concrete.

This patio project follows the steps for building a small (100 square feet or so) slab that can be poured and finished all at once. The patio featured here is a circular, freestanding structure slightly more than 10 ft. in diameter. If you are building a patio of any shape that abuts your house, always isolate it from the house with an isolation board and slope the surface so water drains away from the foundation. A smaller slab is much more manageable for amateurs. Larger slabs often require that you place and tool the wet concrete in workable sections, and these steps must continue simultaneously until the entire slab is filled and leveled before the concrete begins to set. Therefore, it's a good idea to seek guidance and/or assistance from a concrete professional if your plans call for a large patio.

Because they are permanent structures, concrete patios are often governed by local building codes, and you might need a permit for your project—especially if the patio abuts a permanent structure. Before you get started, contact your city's building department to learn about permit requirements and general construction specifications in your area, including:

- Zoning restrictions
- Depth of gravel subbase
- Concrete composition
- Slab thickness and slope
- Internal reinforcement (wire mesh, rebar, etc.)
- Control joints (see page 98)
- Moisture barrier under slab (not a common requirement)

Concrete Coverage ▸

Volume	Slab Thickness	Surface Area
1 cubic yard	2"	160 square feet
1 cubic yard	3"	110 square feet
1 cubic yard	4"	80 square feet
1 cubic yard	5"	65 square feet
1 cubic yard	6"	55 square feet
1 cubic yard	8"	40 square feet

Tools & Materials ▸

Drill	Eye protection	Push broom	Isolation board
Circular saw	Plumb bob	Lumber (1 × 2,	and construction
Hand maul or	Chalk line	2 × 4)	adhesive
sledgehammer	Hammer	Compactable	Concrete form release
Mason's string	Hardboard lap siding	gravel	agent
Stakes	Bolt cutters	Screws	4,000 psi concrete (or
Marking paint	Concrete mixing tools	6 × 6" 10/10 welded	as required by local
Line level	Shovel or masonry hoe	wire mesh	code)
Excavation tools	Wheelbarrow	Tie wire	Clear polyethylene
Bow rake	Bull float	2" wire bolsters	sheeting
Level	Edger	Work gloves	Lawn edger (available
Plate compactor or	1" groover	Square-nose spade	for rent)
hand tamper	Magnesium trowel	Safety protection	

Construction Details

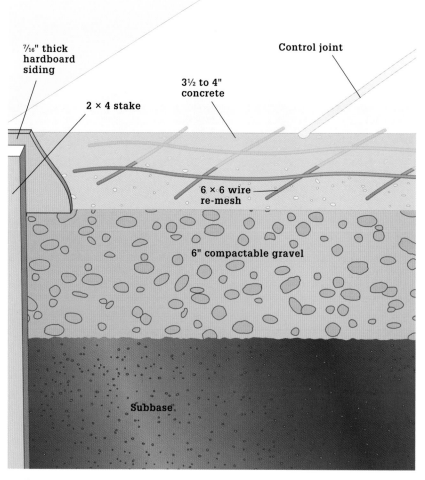

7/16" thick hardboard siding

Control joint

2 × 4 stake

3½ to 4" concrete

6 × 6 wire re-mesh

6" compactable gravel

Subbase

Well-constructed forms and properly-prepared foundational elements will ensure your slab is structurally sound.

When is Concrete Ready to Finish? ▸

Floating wet concrete causes the heavy materials in the mix to sink below the surface, leaving a layer of water—know as bleed water—on the surface. To achieve an attractive and durable finish, let the bleed water disappear before proceeding with the final finishing steps (edging, control joints, and finish troweling). How long this takes depends on the air temperature, humidity, and sun exposure; you just have to watch and wait.

Once the bleed water dries, test the concrete for hardness by stepping on it: if your foot sinks in no more than ¼", the concrete is ready for finishing. Be extra diligent with any areas exposed to the sun or wind, as they can dry much faster than other spots. *Note: Air-entrained concrete (commonly used for cold-weather pours) doesn't show bleed water, so you have to rely on the step test to know when it's time to start finishing.*

How to Build a Round Concrete Patio

Establish layout lines for the site excavation using batterboards, mason's string, and inverted marking paint. Set the lines so they reach at least 12" beyond the work area on all sides. Plan for the gravel base to extend 12" beyond the slab. Use two pairs of perpendicular batterboards with strings to establish the centerpoint of a round patio (where the strings intersect). To create a rough outline for the patio excavation, drive a stake at the centerpoint and then attach a string to the top of the stake. Tape the other end of the string to a can of inverted marking paint so the distance from the stake to the can equals the radius of the circle, including the gravel base; mark the outline.

Cut the sod on the perimeter of the excavation area to define where to dig. For better access, first remove the batterboards (or at least the strings). A lawn edger works well for cutting the outline into the sod (be sure to wear safety equipment).

Story pole

Excavate the site for a 6 to 8"-thick compactable gravel subbase plus any sub-grade (below ground level) portion of the slab. If building next to your house, grade the soil so it slopes away from the house at ⅛" per foot. Measure down from the leveled cross strings with a story pole to gauge the depth as you work. Compact the soil after grading using a plate compactor or a hand tamper.

(continued)

Patio Next to a House ▸

If your patio will butt up to a house or another permanent structure, you should use the house or structure as your starting point for setting slope and establishing a patio layout. Snap a chalk line onto the house foundation at the precise elevation of the top of the finished slab. This should be 1 to 3" below any patio door threshold. You can use this line for reference during the site prep the concrete pour, and finishing.

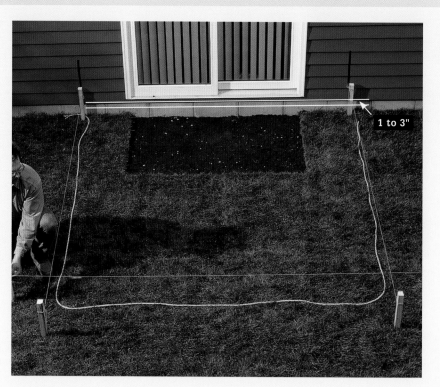

1 to 3"

Fill the excavation area with a 4"-thick layer of compactable gravel. Use an upside-down bow or garden rake to move the rock around. Rake the rock until it is level and follows the grade of the soil base.

Use a plate compactor to tamp the first 4" of graded compactable gravel. Add another 2 to 4" layer of gravel until the top surface will compact to the finished level. Use cross strings and the story pole to make sure the subbase is uniform and follows the ⅛" per ft. slope. Tamp until the gravel is compacted and at the correct height relative to your lines.

6 **Set level lines** for the form height. Replace batterboards and retie the mason's lines so they are level. If you are making a circular patio, as seen here, add intermediate stakes between the batterboards and the tie lines to divide the circle into at least eight segments. Drop a plumb bob from the point where the lines intersect, and drive a stake at this centerpoint. Use this stake to create a string guide and redraw the patio outline (inset).

7 **Drive stakes** for anchoring the forms around the perimeter of the patio, just outside the outline. Drive the stakes deep enough that they will be beneath the tops of the forms. Use a hand maul or sledgehammer to drive the stakes. To prevent them from splitting, use a scrap 2 × 4 as a hammer block to absorb the blows. Drive a stake at each point where a string intersects the patio outline.

8 **Install forms.** Here, 7/16"-thick pieces of hardboard lap siding have been rip-cut into 3½" strips to make bendable forms. Cut each strip long enough to span three stakes as it follows the patio outline. Screw the strip to the middle stake first, making sure the top is the correct distance down from the layout string. Bend the form to follow the outline and attach it to the other stakes.

9 **Drive stakes** behind the forms anywhere where the strips require additional bending or anchoring to follow the round outline. Attach the forms to the stakes. *Note: If you are installing straight 2 × 4 forms, drive screws through the outsides of the stake and into the form boards to make them easier to remove later.*

(continued)

Lay wire mesh over the gravel base, keeping the edges 1 to 2" from the insides of the form. Overlap the mesh strips by 6" and tie them together with tie wire. Prop up the mesh on 2" wire bolsters placed every few feet and tied to the mesh with wire. If required, install isolation board along the house foundation.

Place 4000 psi concrete in the form, starting at the side furthest from the concrete source. Before pouring, construct access ramps so wheelbarrows can roll over the forms without damaging them, and coat the insides of the form with a release agent or vegetable oil to prevent the forms from sticking. Distribute the concrete with a shovel or masonry hoe. As you fill, hammer against the outsides of the forms to eliminate air pockets.

Screed the surface with a long, straight 2 × 4: have two people pull the board backward in a side-to-side sawing motion, with the board resting on top of the form. As you work, shovel in extra concrete to fill the low spots or remove concrete from high spots, and re-screed. The goal is to create a flat surface that's level with the top of the form.

Float the concrete surface with a bull float: without applying pressure, push and pull the float in straight, parallel passes, overlapping each pass slightly with the next. Slightly tip up the leading edge of the float to prevent gouging the surface. Stop floating once the surface is relatively smooth and has a wet sheen. Be careful not to over-float, indicated by water pooling on the surface. Allow the bleed water to disappear.

14

Use an edger to shape all edges of the slab that contact the wood form. Carefully run the edger back and forth along the form to create a smooth, rounded corner. Slightly lift the leading edge of the tool as needed to prevent gouging.

15

Cut a control joint (if required) using a 1" groover guided by a straight 2 × 4. In most cases, you'll need to erect a temporary bridge to allow access for cutting in the center of the patio. Take great care here. Be sure to cut grooves while concrete is still workable. Make several light passes back and forth until the groove reaches full depth, lifting the leading edge of the tool to prevent gouging.

16

Flatten ridges and create a smooth surface with a magnesium trowel. This will create a smooth surface that takes a finish well once the concrete has dried. Another finishing option is simply to skip the additional floating. Then, before the concrete dries completely, brush lightly with a push broom to create a nonslip "broomed" surface.

17

Cure the concrete by misting the slab with water, then covering it with a single piece of polyethylene sheeting. Smooth out any air pockets (which can cause discoloration), and weight the sheeting along the edges. Mist the slab and reapply the plastic daily for 1 to 2 weeks.

Acid-Stained Concrete Patio

Acid staining is a permanent color treatment for cured concrete that yields a translucent, attractively mottled finish ideally suited to patios. Unlike paint or pigmented concrete stains, both of which are surface coatings, acid stain is a chemical solution that soaks into the concrete pores and reacts with the minerals to create the desired color. The color doesn't peel or flake off, and it fades very little over many years. Acid stain won't hide blemishes or discoloration in the original concrete surface, but many consider this an important part of its natural appeal. If your patio or walkway is fully exposed, bear in mind that some colors of acid stain may fade in direct sunlight, so be sure to choose a color guaranteed by the manufacturer not to fade.

You can apply acid stain to new concrete that has cured for at least four to six weeks (check the stain manufacturer's requirements for curing times) or old concrete that is free of any previously applied sealants. Test old concrete by spraying the surface with water: if the water beads on the surface instead of soaking in, there's probably a sealer on there, and it must be removed for good results with the stain. Ask the stain manufacturer for recommended concrete sealer remover products to use.

Another important preparation step with either new or old concrete is to color-test a few shades of stain on the concrete you'll be working with. Stain suppliers often sell sample-size quantities of stain for this purpose. Since acid stain affects every surface a little differently, it's worth the effort to run a test before committing to a color. Be sure to test in an inconspicuous area, because the stain can't be removed once it's applied.

Tools & Materials ▸

Tape	Eye protection
Plastic sheeting	NIOSH/MSHA-
Stiff-bristled brush	approved respirator
Concrete cleaner	Cleaner/neutralizer
and solvent	Medium-bristled
All-plastic garden	scrub brush
sprayer	Towel
Stain	Sealer
Protective clothing	

Acid-staining a patio is a fairly simple procedure that can be done by almost everyone. Be sure the surface is completely cured, clean (use water, not soap), and dry; and be sure to wear the protective gear, as recommended by the manufacturer. A properly maintained acid-stained patio can last forever.

How to Apply an Acid Stain

Protect all surfaces adjacent to the concrete and any nearby plants with tape and plastic sheeting.

Clean the entire surface with an approved cleaner and stiff-bristled brush. Mix the stain with water in an all-plastic garden sprayer, as directed. Use an approved solvent to remove undesirable markings on the concrete surface (stain won't hide them). Rinse thoroughly and then let dry.

Spray the stain onto the concrete using random circular motions and holding the spray tip about 18" from the surface. Work backward from one side. Maintain pressure on the sprayer so the spray pattern is consistently fine and even. Wet the surface completely, but avoid creating puddles. Allow the first coat of stain to dry completely.

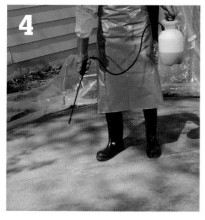

Apply a second coat using the same technique. Darker tones will appear with the second coat; the wetter the surface, the darker the tones will be (but again, avoid puddles of stain). Let the second coat dry completely.

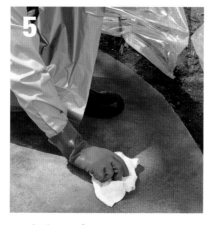

Wash the surface using a recommended cleaner/neutralizer and a medium-bristled scrub brush to remove dried stain residue. Thoroughly rinse according to the manufacturer's instructions. Test-wipe the surface with a white towel: If the towel shows stain, wash and rinse the surface again.

Apply sealer using a high-quality deck/patio sprayer (or other recommended applicator). Follow the manufacturer's instructions and recommendations—most sealers require multiple coats. Maintain even pressure on the sprayer for a consistently fine spray. Wet the surface completely with a thin coating, and avoid puddles. Let the sealer dry between coats.

Warning ▸

Always pour acid stain into water; never pour water into acid stain.

Working with Concrete ▸

Estimating concrete can be done with a simple calculation. Concrete quantity is measured in cubic yards. To calculate the volume of concrete needed for your project, simply follow these steps:

1. Multiply the width and length of the slab (in feet) to find the total square footage. For example: 10 ft. (width) × 12 ft. (length) = 120 sq. ft.
2. Convert the thickness dimension of the slab to feet by dividing by 12. For example: 4" (slab thickness) ÷ 12 = 0.33 feet.
3. Multiply the square footage by the thickness to find the cubic volume in feet, then divide by 27 to find the cubic yard volume: 120 × 0.33 = 39.6 cu. ft. 39.6 ÷ 27 = 1.47 cu. yd.

When estimating concrete needs, it's best to round up to the nearest half increment to make sure you don't run short. Therefore, for a slab volume of 1.25 cubic yards, purchase or order at least 1.5 yards of concrete.

Isolation joints prevent the wet concrete from bonding to the adjoining structure and act as a cushion to prevent damage if any seasonal movement occurs. The standard material for slab isolation joints is ½"-thick asphalt-impregnated fiberboard. The board should be glued or nailed to the adjoining structure prior to the concrete pour. After the new concrete has cured, trim off the top ½" or so of the isolation board and fill the joint with a suitable masonry caulk, if desired.

A control joint works somewhat like a fault line: because cracking is a normal occurrence with slabs, the joint creates a weak spot in the structure, encouraging cracks to follow the joint (where they are less visible).

Consult your local building department for recommendations and requirements for control joint frequency and placement. In general, a control joint groove should equal a quarter of the total slab thickness (for example, a 4"-thick slab gets 1"-deep joints). For best performance and appearance, arrange control joints in a symmetrical grid pattern, dividing the slab into roughly equal square sections. For large slabs, control joints are typically required every 8 to 12 feet. Joints in concrete walkways are typically spaced at one-and-a-half times the width of the walkway sections (for example, a 2-foot-wide walkway should have a control joint every 3 feet).

Isolation joints are required wherever a new concrete slab abuts a permanent structure, such as a house foundation, a wall, or another concrete slab.

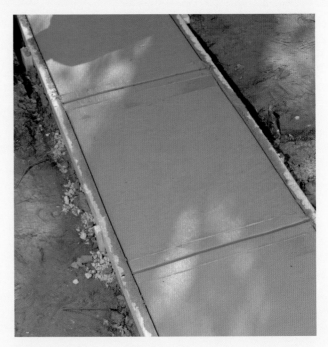

Control joints are permanent, straight grooves cut into the top surface of concrete slabs during the finishing process.

When mixing your own concrete, work with premixed dry concrete. It is commonly sold in 60- and 80-lb. bags. Using premixed concrete ensures you get the right formulation for quality results. There are several types of premixed concrete, each with specific properties—such as fiber-reinforced or high-early-strength—so choose the formulation that best suits your application.

A 60-lb. bag of concrete mix yields roughly half a cubic foot of solid concrete. For a patio slab, the number of bags required adds up quickly. If you're planning a sizable slab that must be poured all at once, or any job requiring at least a cubic yard of concrete, you're better off ordering ready-mix (see below). For small jobs, you can mix a couple of bags at a time in a mortar box or wheelbarrow. For larger projects, consider renting a power concrete mixer.

Follow the manufacturer's instructions carefully when mixing the concrete. Most manufacturers recommend mixing in just half of the water to start with, then adding more water incrementally until the proper consistency is achieved. If mixed too dry, the concrete will be difficult to work; if too wet, the strength of the finished surface is compromised.

Ready-mix concrete is ordered and professionally delivered for jobs that call for one cubic yard or more. Here are some tips for ordering concrete for your project:

- Discuss your project with the experts at the ready-mix company. They will help you determine how much and what type of concrete you need.
- Be prepared for the pour, with a well-secured form, all the necessary tools, and plenty of helpers. Last-minute changes or a "wing it" attitude can lead to disastrous results with poured concrete.
- Establish a clear delivery path to the project site. Lay down a walkway of wood planks for wheelbarrow travel over grass and soft materials. Make sure the truck has plenty of room to park without damaging your property.
- Call the ready-mix company the day before the scheduled pour to confirm the quantity and delivery time.
- Read the receipt you get from the driver: it gives the time the batch was mixed. Before you accept the delivery, make sure no more than 90 minutes have elapsed between the mixing and delivery times.

To mix concrete with a power mixer, fill a bucket with ½ gallon of clean water for each 60-lb. bag of dry mix (three bags is workable for most mixers). Pour in ½ of the water, and then add all of the dry ingredients. Mix for 1 minute. Add water as needed to reach the desired consistency, then mix for 3 minutes. Empty the mix into a wheelbarrow, and rinse the drum immediately.

To mix concrete by hand, pour dry mix from bags into a mortar box or wheelbarrow. Pour in ½ gallon of clean water for each 60-lb. bag of mix. Work the mixture with a mason's hoe or garden hoe, carefully adding water to achieve the desired consistency. Do not overwork the mix.

Ready-mix may cost more than premixed bags, but it's much faster for large projects, and there's no guesswork in getting the right consistency. Many ready-mix companies have a 1-yard minimum for delivery orders.

Seeded Concrete & Wood Patio

A poured concrete patio divided by wood forms is an attractive alternative to a monolithic concrete slab. In addition to its decorative appearance, this type of surface is easier to create, since the permanent forms divide the concrete pour into four equal sections (or more, as desired). Each section can be poured and finished before moving on to the next, or you can complete all the quadrants in a day. If you choose the latter, you must watch the poured quadrants carefully and finish them at the proper time, so you'll need a couple of helpers. As an optional addition, this project includes steps for seeding the concrete with small stones, or seeding aggregate, introducing color and texture to the concrete surface.

The form lumber used in the project is brown, pressure-treated 2 × 4s, chosen because it's more attractive than most green-treated wood. If green is all you can find, you can color the wood with a compatible stain. In any case, use high-quality lumber rated for ground contact, and avoid the type with visible incise marks on the surface, a result of certain forms of treatment. For bolder grid lines, you can use 4 × 4 lumber instead of 2 × 4, joining the form pieces with galvanized spikes.

Tools & Materials ▶

Rope or hose
Mason's string
Excavation tools
Hand tamp or plate
  compactor
Wheelbarrow
Masonry hoe
Magnesium float
Wood concrete float
Concrete edger
Stiff-bristled brush
Paint roller
Stakes
Compactable gravel
Pressure-treated
  2 × 4 lumber
6 × 6" [10/10]
  welded wire mesh
2" wire bolsters

Concrete mix
Seeding aggregate
Polyethylene
  sheeting
Concrete sealer
Eye and ear
  protection
Square-nose spade
Scrap 2 × 2 lumber
Galvanized deck
  screws (2½", 4")
Masking tape
Heavy-duty wire
  cutters
Hammer
Gloves and particle
  mask
Circular saw

This four-square patio replaced a small, crumbling slab that had become an eyesore. The new patio combines pressure-treated wood with aggregate to create a natural-looking, durable surface.

Construction Details

This divided concrete patio includes 4"-thick concrete slabs reinforced internally with 6 × 6" 10/10 welded wire mesh. The mesh is supported by 2" wire bolsters to keep it near the middle of the slab interior. The patio, including the forms, is built upon a 6" subbase of compacted gravel. When planning your patio project, consult your local building department to learn about the following requirements:

- Zoning restrictions
- Depth of gravel subbase
- Concrete composition
- Slab thickness and slope
- Internal reinforcement (wire mesh, rebar, etc.)
- Moisture barrier under slab

Adapt the project as shown to meet the local requirements. For additional information on working with concrete, see pages 88 to 95 and 98 to 99.

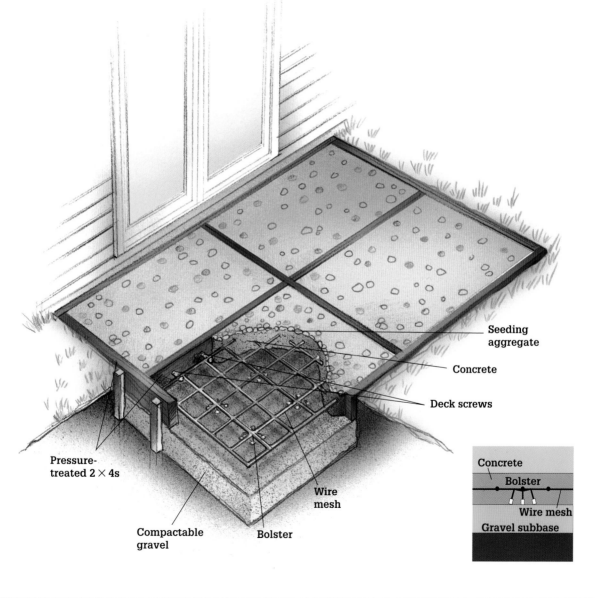

Seeding aggregate

Concrete

Deck screws

Wire mesh

Bolster

Compactable gravel

Pressure-treated 2 × 4s

Concrete
Bolster
Wire mesh
Gravel subbase

How to Build a Seeded Concrete & Wood Patio

Prepare the building site by removing any existing building materials, such as for a sidewalk or landing area. If the new patio will abut the house foundation under a patio door, plan to make the height of the finished surface 1 to 3" below the door threshold.

Lay out the rough position of the patio using a rope or hose, then mark the exact layout with stakes and mason's strings. Set the strings for a ¼"-per-ft. downward slope away from the foundation (see pages 40 to 45 for detailed steps on site layout and preparation).

Remove sod and excavate the project area to a consistent depth using mason's strings attached to stakes for reference. Mark the excavation depth onto a story pole, and use it to make sure the excavation is a uniform distance from the strings at all points.

Create a subbase for the patio by filling the site with an even 3" layer of compactable gravel and tamp the gravel with a hand tamp or rented plate compactor. Add more gravel for a total base thickness of 6" after compaction. Grade the gravel to follow the slope of the layout and tamp thoroughly.

Cut pressure-treated 2 × 4 boards to build a permanent frame that outlines the entire patio site. Lay the boards in place using mason's strings as guides. Fasten the ends together with 2½" galvanized deck screws. Temporarily stake the forms at 2-ft. intervals, set a straight 2 × 4 across the side forms, and set a level on top of the 2 × 4 to check the side forms for level. *Tip: Wear gloves and a particle mask when cutting pressure-treated lumber.*

Cut and install pressure-treated 2 × 4s to divide the square into quadrants; cut one piece full length, and attach two one-half length pieces to it with screws driven toenail style. Drive 4" deck screws partway into the forms every 12" at inside locations. The portions that stick out will act as tie rods between the poured concrete and the permanent forms. *Tip: Protect the tops of the permanent forms by covering them with masking tape.*

Cut reinforcing wire mesh to fit inside each quadrant, leaving 1" clearance on all sides. Mix concrete and pour the quadrants one at a time, starting with the one located farthest from the concrete source. Use a masonry hoe to spread the concrete evenly in the forms.

Smooth off the concrete with a straight 2 × 4 screed board that rests on the forms. Settle the concrete by sliding a spade along the inside edges of the forms and rapping the outer edges of the forms with a hammer.

(continued)

Allow bleed water to disappear, and then spread clean seeding aggregate evenly over the surface by hand or with a shovel. *Note: if you're using small aggregate (up to 1" in diameter), spread it out in a single layer; for larger aggregate, maintain a separation between stones that is roughly equal to the size of the stone.*

Pat the aggregate down with the screed board, then float the surface with a magnesium float until a thin layer of concrete covers the stones. Do not overfloat. If bleed water appears, stop floating and let it dry before completing the step. If you are seeding a large area, cover it with polyethylene sheeting to keep the concrete from hardening too quickly.

Cut along the edges of the quadrant with a concrete edger, then use a wood float to smooth out any marks left behind by the tool.

Option: If you have enough help and your project is small enough, you may want to pour remaining quadrants at this time, repeating steps 7 through 11. Be sure to check poured quadrants periodically: if the surface water has evaporated from the concrete, uncover the quadrants and proceed to step 12.

After all the water has evaporated from the concrete surface, expose the aggregate by misting the surface with water and scrubbing the surface with a stiff-bristled brush. Remove the protective tape from the forms, then recover the quadrants with sheeting and let the concrete cure for one week.

After the concrete has cured, rinse and scrub the aggregate again to clean off any remaining residue. *Tip: Use diluted muriatic acid to wash off stubborn concrete residue. Read manufacturer's instructions for mixing rations and safety precautions.*

After three weeks, seal the patio surface with exposed-aggregate sealer. Reapply sealer periodically as needed, following the manufacturer's recommendations.

Tiled Concrete Slab

Outdoor tile can be made of several different materials and is available in many colors and styles. Using natural stone tiles with different shapes and complementary colors, as demonstrated in this project, is a great way to draw attention to the elegant surface. Tile manufacturers may offer brochures giving you ideas for modular patterns that can be created from their tiles. Make sure the tiles you select are intended for outdoor use.

When laying a modular, geometric pattern with tiles of different sizes, it's crucial that you test the layout before you begin and that you place the first tiles very carefullly. The first tiles will dictate the placement of all other tiles in your layout.

You can pour a new concrete slab on which to install your tile patio (see pages 88 to 95), but another option is to finish an existing slab by veneering it with tile—the scenario shown here.

Outdoor tile must be installed on a clean, flat and stable surface. When tiling an existing concrete slab, the surface must be free of flaking, wide cracks, and other major imperfections. A damaged slab can be repaired by applying a one- to two-inch-thick layer of new concrete over the old surface before laying tile.

Tools & Materials ▸

Tape measure	Buckets
Pencil	Paint roller
Chalk line	Plastic sheeting
Tile cutter or wet saw	Thin-set mortar
Tile nippers	Modular tile
square-notched trowel	Grout
2 × 4 padded with carpet	Grout additive
Hammer	Grout sealer
Grout float	Tile sealer
Grout sponge	Ear and eye protection
Caulk gun	Work gloves
Tile spacers	Mason's trowel
	Cloth
	Foam brush

Note: Wear eye protection when cutting tile, handle cut tiles carefully—the cut edges of some materials may be very sharp.

Stone tiles can be laid as veneer over a concrete patio slab—a very easy way to create an elegant patio.

Tile options for landscape installations: Slate and other smooth, natural stone materials are durable and blend well with any landscape, but are usually expensive. Quarry tile is less expensive, though only available in limited colors. Exterior-rated porcelain or ceramic tiles are moderately priced and available in a wide range of colors and textures, with many styles imitating the look of natural stone. Terra cotta tile is made from molded clay for use in warm, dry climates only. Many of these materials require application of a sealer to increase durability and prevent staining and moisture penetration.

Slate · Cut stone · Terra-cotta tile · Quarry tile · Ceramic tile

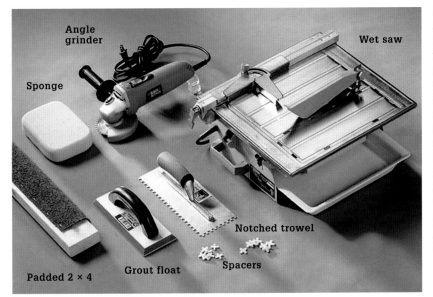

Exterior tile installation tools include: a wet saw for cutting tile quickly and easily (available at rental centers—make certain to rent one that is big enough for the tile size you install), an angle grinder with a diamond-edged cutting blade (also a rental item) for cutting curves or other complex contours, a trowel with square notches (of the size required for your tile size) for spreading the mortar adhesive, spacers for accurate aligning of tiles and setting consistent joint widths, a straight length of 2 × 4 padded along one edge (carpet pad works well) for helping align tile surfaces, a grout float for spreading grout to fill the joints, and a sponge for cleaning excess grout from tile surfaces.

Angle grinder · Sponge · Wet saw · Notched trowel · Grout float · Spacers · Padded 2 × 4

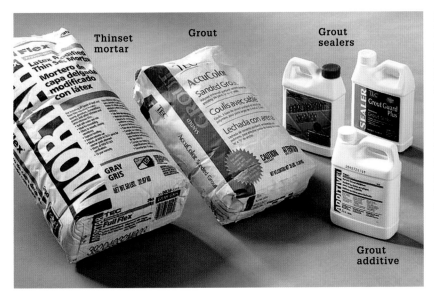

Exterior tile installation materials include: latex-modified thin set mortar adhesive that is mixed with water (if you can't find thinset that is latex modified, buy unmodified thinset and mix it with a latex additive for mortar following manufacturer's directions), exterior-rated grout available in a variety of colors to match the tile you use, grout additive to improve durability, grout sealer to help protect grout from moisture and staining, and tile sealer required for some tile materials (follow tile manufacturer's requirements).

Thinset mortar · Grout · Grout sealers · Grout additive

Evaluating Concrete Surfaces

A good surface is free from any major cracks or badly flaking concrete (called spalling). You can apply patio tile directly over a concrete surface that is in good condition if it has control joints (see below).

A fair surface may exhibit minor cracking and spalling but has no major cracks or badly deteriorated spots. Install a new concrete subbase over a surface in fair condition before laying patio tile.

A poor surface contains deep or large cracks, broken, sunken, or heaved concrete, or extensive spalling. If you have this kind of surface, remove the concrete completely and replace it with a new concrete slab before you lay patio tile.

Cutting Control Joints in a Concrete Patio

Control joint

Control joint location

Cut new control joints into existing concrete patios that are in good condition but do not have enough control joints. Control joints allow inevitable cracking to occur in locations that don't weaken the concrete or detract from its appearance. They should be cut every 5 or 6 ft. in a patio. Plan the control joints so they will be below tile joints once the tile layout is established (photo, above right). Use a circular saw with a masonry blade set to ⅜" depth to cut control joints. Cover the saw base with duct tape to prevent it from being scratched.

How to Tile a Patio Slab

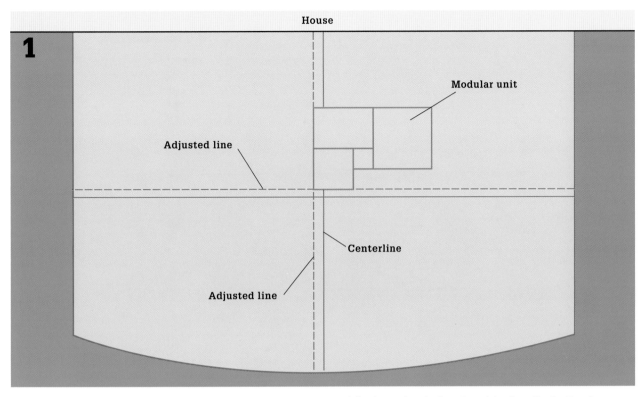

To establish a layout for tile with a modular pattern, you must carefully determine the location of the first tile. On the clean and dry concrete surface, measure and mark a centerline down the center of the slab. Test-fit tiles along the line—because of the modular pattern used here, the tiles are staggered. Mark the edge of a tile nearest the center of the pad, then create a second line perpendicular to the first and test-fit tiles along this line.

Make adjustments as needed so the modular pattern breaks evenly over the patio surface and is symmetrical from side to side. You may need to adjust the position of one or both lines. The intersection of the lines is where your tile installation will begin. Outline the position of each group of tiles on the slab.

(continued)

Variation: To establish a traditional grid pattern, test-fit rows of tiles so they run in each direction, intersecting at the center of the patio. Adjust the layout to minimize tile cutting at the sides and ends, then mark the final layout and snap chalk lines across the patio to create four quadrants. As you lay tile, work along the chalk lines and in one quadrant at a time.

Following manufacturer's instructions, mix enough thinset mortar to work for about 2 hours (start with 4 to 5" deep in a 5-gallon bucket). At the intersection of the two layout lines, use a notched-edge trowel to spread thinset mortar over an area large enough to accommodate the layout of the first modular group of tiles. Hold the trowel at a 45° angle to rake the mortar to a consistent depth.

Set the first tile, twisting it slightly as you push it into the mortar. Align it with both adjusted layout lines, then place a padded 2 × 4 over the center of the tile and give it a light rap with a hammer to set the tile.

Position the second tile adjacent to the first with a slight gap between them. Place spacers on end in the joint near each corner and push the second tile against the spacers. Make certain the first tile remains aligned with the layout lines. Set the padded 2 × 4 across both tiles and tap to set. Use a damp cloth to remove any mortar that squeezes out of the joint or gets on tile surfaces. Joints must be at least ⅛"-deep to hold grout.

Lay the remaining tiles of the first modular unit using spacers. Using the trowel, scrape the excess mortar from the concrete slab in areas you will not yet be working on to prevent it from hardening and interfering with the installation.

With the first modular unit set, continue laying tile following the pattern established. You can use the chalk lines for general reference, but they will not be necessary as layout lines. To prevent squeeze-out between tiles, scrape a heavy accumulation of mortar ½" away from the edge of a set tile before setting the adjacent tile.

Cutting Curves in Tile ▸

To make convex (left) or concave (right) curves, mark the profile of the curve on the tile, then use a wet saw to make parallel straight cuts, each time cutting as close to the marked line as possible. Use a tile nippers to break off small portions of tabs, gradually working down to the curve profile. Finally, use an angle grinder to smooth off the sharp edges of the tabs. Make sure to wear a particle mask when using the tile saw and wear sturdy gloves when using the nippers.

(continued)

After installing the tile, cover the tiled area with plastic, and let the thinset mortar cure according to the manufacturer's instructions. When tile has fully set, remove the plastic and mix grout, using a grout additive instead of water. Grout additive is especially important in outdoor applications, because it creates joints that are more resilient in changing temperatures.

Use a grout float to spread grout over an area that is roughly 10 sq. ft. Push down with the face of the float to force grout into the joints, then hold the float edge at a 45° angle to the tile surface and scrape off the excess grout.

Once you've grouted this area, wipe off the grout residue using a damp sponge. Wipe with a light, circular motion—you want to clean tile surfaces without pulling grout out of the joints. Don't try to get the tile perfectly clean the first time. Wipe the area several times, rinsing out the sponge frequently.

11

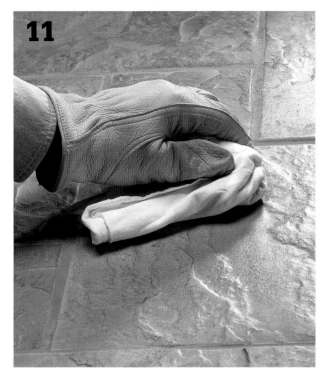

Once the grout has begun to set (usually about 1 hour, depending on temperature and humidity), clean the tile surfaces again. You want to thoroughly clean grout residue from tile surfaces because it is difficult to remove once it has hardened. Buff off a light film left after final cleaning with a cloth.

Grouting Porous Tiles ▶

Some tiles, such as slate, have highly porous surfaces that can be badly stained by grout. For these tiles, apply grout by filling an empty caulk tube (available at tile stores and some building centers) with grout, and apply the grout to the joints with a caulk gun. Cut the tip to make an opening just large enough to allow grout to be forced out. Run the tip down the joint between tiles as you squeeze out the grout. Remove the grout that gets on the tile surface with a wet sponge. You may need to use your finger to force grout into the joint—protect your skin by wearing a heavy glove to do this.

12

Cover the pad with plastic and let the grout cure according to manufacturer's instructions. Once the grout has cured, use a foam brush to apply grout sealer to only the grout, wiping any spillover off of tile surfaces.

13

Apply tile sealer to the entire surface using a paint roller. Cover the patio with plastic and allow the sealer to dry completely before exposing the patio to weather or traffic.

Loose Materials Patio

Gravel, crushed stone, wood chips, and other loose materials are very easy to install and are a surprisingly attractive patio surface. The versatile nature of loose material lends itself to everything from creative mixed-media designs to plain surfaces that evoke the simple beauty of Zen rock gardens.

The basic installation of a loose materials patio starts with excavating the site, then adding a two-inch layer of compacted gravel and edging material. Edging is required for this project to contain the loose surface material. From this point, the installation depends on the type of material you're using.

For crushed stone, gravel, and other small aggregates, add one to two inches of surface material and tamp flat; for river rock, add two inches or more (based on rock size); for wood chips, add at least a two-inch-thick layer and rake smooth.

For the smoothest, hardest surface, use a highly compactable material, such as decomposed granite (DG), for the finish material—or you can cover a coarser gravel base with granite fines (rock dust). Compact either surface with a plate compactor.

Tools & Materials ▸

Drill	2½" drywall screws
Circular saw	Professional-grade
Sledgehammer	landscape fabric
Mason's string	Compactable gravel
Line level	Edging
Excavation tools	Gravel or other fill
Bow rake	material
Plate compactor	Eye and ear
Plumb bob	protection
Lumber (2 × 2,	Work gloves
2 × 4)	

A loose material patio provides a casual, natural environment for any type of patio. The footing is not as solid underfoot, so it is best used where that is not a concern.

How to Create a Loose Material Patio

Plan and excavate the site. Lay out the patio site with batterboards and mason's strings, planning for a slope of ⅛" per foot (see pages 40 to 45 for detailed steps on layout and site preparation). Excavate the site to a depth of 4" (or as desired, depending on the surface material and your application), and tamp the soil with a plate compactor. Cover the site with landscape fabric, overlapping the edges by at least 6".

Add compactable gravel and edging: cover the site with compactable gravel, rake it flat and smooth, and then tamp it thoroughly with a plate compactor. The layer should be about 2" thick after compaction. Install patio edging as desired, setting it at least ½" higher than the top of the finished patio surface to help contain the surface material.

Option: Install accent pavers. Set pavers (stone, concrete, wood, or other material) onto the gravel base, as desired. For flagstone and other materials that might not be flat on the bottom, add sand underneath to prevent wobbling.

Spread out the surface material over the patio area, raking it into an even layer of the desired thickness.

Tamp the surface material, if appropriate, with a hand tamp, plate compactor, or drum roller to create an even, flat surface. If the surface material is stone or other masonry, spray the patio with water to wash away dirt and dust.

Loose-fill Patio with Fire Pit

A fire pit makes a wonderful focal point for backyard gatherings. Many local codes stipulate that a fire pit area should be at least 20 feet across, including the surrounding circular area that can be outfitted with chairs and benches. Dressed with rock (trap rock is shown here), this area creates a safety zone between the pit and structures or combustible yard elements, such as landscape plants and dry lawns. For comfort and safety, fire pits should be installed only on level ground. If your proposed seating area is on a slope, you can build a retaining wall (see pages 51 to 55) on the high side, and the wall itself can provide another surface for seating or setting down plates and drinks.

The fire pit featured here is constructed around a metal liner that you can buy from landscape supply centers. A liner will keep the fire pit wall from overheating and cracking if cooled suddenly by rain or a bucket of water. The liner seen here is a section of 36"-diameter corrugated culvert pipe. Other types of suitable liners are often sold as "barbecue rings" or "fire rings." Typically made of steel or iron, rings may include integral grills or have flanges for setting in a removable barbecue grate. The wall of the fire pit in this project is built with ashlar stones that are relatively uniform in size and have flat sides that make for easy stacking. But you can use any type of stone you like, as well as cast concrete retaining wall blocks. Whatever material you choose, set the wall stones on a solid foundation of compactable gravel, as with a paver patio. It's most efficient to prep the base for the seating area at the same time as the fire pit.

Tools & Materials ▸

Wheelbarrow	Metal fire pit liner
Marking paint	Compactable gravel
Excavation tools	Dressing rock
Hand tamp	Wall stones
Plate compactor	Rake
Level	Eye and ear
Straight 2 × 4	protection
Hand maul or	Work gloves
sledgehammer	Stakes
1"-dia. pipe	Square-nose spade
Landscape edging	

A loose-fill patio and stone fire pit is what you'd expect to find in the Old West or on trails deep in the forest. Why not bring this to your backyard? It's a simple DIY project that incorporates a compactable gravel foundation topped with a decorative rock or loose stone material and an excavated area reserved for the fire pit.

Construction Details

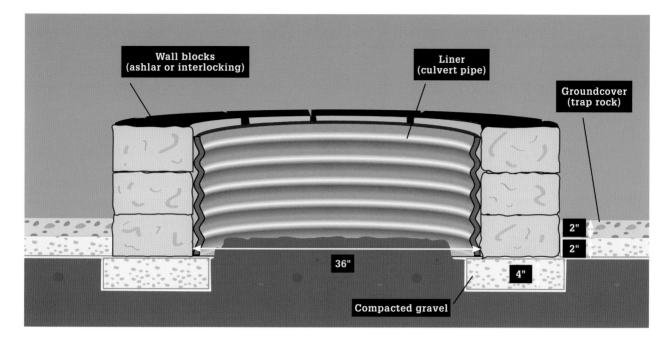

Wall blocks (ashlar or interlocking)

Liner (culvert pipe)

Groundcover (trap rock)

2"

2"

36"

4"

Compacted gravel

How to Build a Loose-fill Patio with Fire Pit

Mark the patio outline: drive a length of pipe into the center of the pit area. Measure out from the pipe a distance equal to the outside radius of the seating area. Use a cord with a loop in it and a can of marking paint to draw a circle with this radius onto the ground around the pipe.

Cut out the sod and excavate the site to a level plane 4" below grade (or as appropriate for the surface material) over the entire circled area, from pipe to perimeter (leave the pipe in place for now).

(continued)

Excavate the fire pit wall area. Draw two more circles around the center pipe: an inner circle with a radius 6" smaller than the radius of the pit liner and an outer circle with a radius 6" larger than the outside radius of the finished fire pit. These lines mark the base for supporting the wall stones. Excavate an additional 4" down within this ring and compact the soil at the bottom of the trench with a hand tamp.

Fill the trench with compactable gravel and tamp it thoroughly so it is very hard. Fill the entire patio area with compactable gravel to 2" below grade. Use a level on a straight 2 × 4 to flatten and level the gravel (the area in the wall trench must be perfectly flat and level. Do not compact the top layer of gravel.

Position the metal fire pit liner so it is centered around the pipe and is perfectly level. Add or remove gravel beneath to level the liner, as needed.

Lay the first course of wall stones around the liner. Adjust the stones so they maintain a consistent spacing to the liner and between one another. Check with a level as you work to make sure the stones are level across the top.

7

Lay the remaining courses of wall stones, staggering the vertical joints between courses. If desired, top the fire pit wall with a cap row of smooth, flat stones. The top of the wall should be at least slightly higher than the edge of the liner.

8

Compact the gravel in the surrounding area with a plate compactor. This will stabilize the area and form a hard subbase that inhibits weed growth. Install the edging of your choice along the perimeter of the loose fill area.

9

Add a 2"-layer of top-dressing rock in the seating area, raking it flat and level. Compact the layer with a plate compactor. *Tip: Angular rock, such as the trap rock seen here, makes a better walking surface than smooth, rounded gravel.*

Wood Tile Patio

Wood patio tiles, also called *deck tiles* or *decking tiles*, are manufactured units made with wood slats and a plastic or rubber backing. Some tiles snap together, while others are simply laid down and held in place by your own border or edge treatment. Some manufacturers offer decorative edge strips for finishing the edges and corners, as well as tapered reducer strips for easing the transition between the tile and concrete surfaces. Tiles are commonly available in 12 and 24" squares, making it easy to plan your layout before purchasing. You can also cut the tiles to suit your layout or fit around obstructions.

Tools & Materials ▸

Wood tile	Tape measure
Cardboard	Chalk line
Jigsaw with down-cutting wood blade	Rubber mats or tiles
	Straightedge
	Utility knife
Corrosion-resistant screws	Eye and ear protection
Drill	Clamps
Sandpaper	Work gloves

Wood patio tiles are made of wood slats held together by an underlying plastic mat or internal tubing. The slats are affixed with screws or staples. This product offers all the warmth and character of decks or wooden floors for an enhanced outdoor living experience.

How to Cover a Patio with Wood Tiles

Set out a full row of tiles according to the desired pattern, starting at one corner of the patio, to see how the tiles lay out. If cuts are required along the sides, start your layout in the center so the cut pieces will be equal on both side edges. With the layout determined, begin setting the tiles (and border pieces, if applicable).

Create cardboard templates to mark tiles for cutting to fit around corners and obstructions. Make the template blanks the same size as an installed tile. Mark and cut each blank as needed until the template fits neatly around the obstruction. Set the template over a tile and trace along the cutout portion with a pencil.

Cut tiles with a jigsaw fitted with a down-cutting wood blade. This allows you to cut from the top side of the tile without splintering the edges. Follow the pencil marks to complete the cut.

Secure any loose slat ends (resulting from the cut) to the support base using corrosion-resistant screws (stainless steel are best). Drive the screws through the base and into the bottom face of the slat(s). Sand the cut edges, and install the tile. Lay the remaining tiles to complete the patio.

Rubber Tile Patio

Rubber pavers are available in large mats and individual paver units. For quick patio upgrades, mats are generally the easiest and least expensive option. Covering a patio with mats couldn't be easier, and the surface is maintenance-free, aside from a quick hose-down to keep it clean. Because of the friction between rubber and concrete (in addition to the weight of the mats), paver mats don't need perimeter edging to stay in place. The rubber material is also more comfortable underfoot than concrete and other hard surfaces—a nice feature for outdoor cooks who spend a lot of time standing at the grill. When choosing rubber paver mats, look for products with good UV resistance and a nonslip, textured surface. Some mats are made with recycled rubber, a decidedly green option for this modern patio treatment.

Tools & Materials ▸

Cardboard
Jigsaw with down-cutting wood blade
Corrosion-resistant screws
Drill
Sand paper
Tape measure
Chalk line
Rubber mats or tiles
Straightedge
Utility knife
Eye and ear protection
Clamps
Work gloves

Rubber tiles typically fit together in a tongue-and-groove system. They have an almost mesh underlayment that allows for drainage as well as ventilation. Rubber tiles are often recycled, but there are many similar tile products of various hardness, size, color, and material available.

How to Cover a Patio with Rubber Mats or Tiles

Create a layout for the installation by measuring the patio (or using the mats themselves) and snapping one or more chalk lines for reference. Determine which edges of the patio will look best with full mats and which will have cut pieces. Typically, it's best to install full mats outward from the center so that cut mats along the side edges of the patio are roughly equal on both sides. If this layout yields cut mats smaller than half a mat, shift the layout so the centerline bisects full mats rather than following a seam. When you're satisfied with the layout, snap a chalk line to guide the first row of mats at or near the patio's center.

Position mats along the reference line, following the desired pattern. Complete any full-mat rows, such as along the house wall or front edge of the patio. Align the remaining mats, letting any cut rows run long until all of the mats are in place.

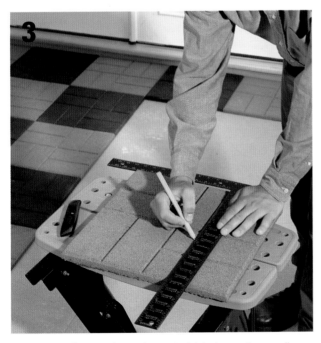

Mark mats for cutting using a straightedge and a pencil.

Cut the mats with a sharp utility knife and a straightedge. Start with a careful scoring cut, then make a few more passes to cut through the material. Lay the mats in place as you cut them to complete the installation.

Patio Edging

Edging can play many different roles in patio and walkway design. Its most practical purpose is containment—keeping the surface material in place so paving doesn't drift off into the yard. As a decorative feature, edging creates a visual border that adds a sense of order or closure to the path or patio space. This effect can be enhanced by edging with a material that contrasts with the surface material or can be made more subtle by using the same material, perhaps in a slightly different pattern. Finally, edging can serve to strengthen the patio or walkway as a hard, protective curb that stands up to years of foot traffic.

The best time to install edging depends on your application. For most sandset paving and loose material surfaces, edging is typically installed on top of the compacted gravel subbase. Edging along existing concrete slabs can be applied on top of the slab or along the sides, with the proper order determined by the finish materials.

To minimize the number of cuts required for paving, install edging after the patio surface is complete. You can also install two adjacent sides of edging to form a right angle, providing an accurate guide for starting the paver pattern, and then install the remaining two sides up against the laid pavers. A third option is to set up temporary 2 × 4 edging, which can be easily replaced with the real thing after the paving is finished.

Install professional-grade paver edging along chalk lines (chalk lines are snapped directly below the outlines you've created with the mason's strings). The paver edge should rest on the compacted gravel.

Rigid Paver Edging

Choose heavy-duty edging that's strong enough to contain your surface materials. If your patio or walkway has curves, buy plenty of notched, or flexible, edging for the curves. Also, buy 12"-long galvanized spikes: one for every 12" of edging plus extra for curves.

Tools & Materials ▸

Maul
Snips or saw (for
    cutting edging)

Heavy-duty plastic
    edging
12" galvanized spikes

Invisible Edging ▸

Invisible edging is so named for its low-profile edge that stops about halfway up the side edges of pavers. The exposed portion of the edging is easily concealed under soil and sod or groundcover.

Rigid plastic edging installs easily and works well for both curved and straight walkways made from paving stones or brick pavers set in sand.

Brick pavers

Sand

Rigid
plastic
edging

Landscape fabric

Compactable gravel subbase

How to Install Rigid Paver Edging

Set the edging on top of a compacted gravel base covered with landscape fabric. Using your layout strings as guides, secure the edging with spikes driven every 12" (or as recommended by the manufacturer). Along curves, spike the edging at every tab, or as recommended.

Cover the outside of the edging with soil and/or sod after the paving is complete. *Tip: On two or more sides of the patio or path, you can spike the edging minimally, in case you have to make adjustments during the paving. Anchor the edging completely after the paving is done.*

Brick Paver Edging

Brick edging can be laid in several different configurations (see below): on-end with its edge perpendicular to the paved surface ("soldiers"); on its long edges; or laid flat, either parallel or perpendicular to the paving. For mortared surfaces, brick can also be mortared to the edge of a concrete slab for a decorative finish (see pages 70 to 73 and 160 to 163).

Tools & Materials ▸

Flat shovel
Rubber mallet
2 × 4 (about 12" long)
Bricks
Hand tamper

Garden spade
Work gloves
Gravel
Landscape fabric
Eye protection

Brick Edging Configurations ▸

Brick soldier edging

Brick set on long edges

Brick set on faces, perpendicular or parallel to the patio surface

How to Install Brick Paver Edging

Excavate the edge of the patio or walkway site using a flat shovel to create a clean, vertical edge. The edge of the soil (and sod) will support the outsides of the bricks. For edging with bricks set on-end, dig a narrow trench along the perimeter of the site, setting the depth so the tops of the edging bricks will be flush with the paving surface (or just above the surface for loose materials).

Set the edging bricks into the trench after installing the gravel subbase and landscape fabric. If applicable, use your layout strings to keep the bricks in line and to check for the proper height. Backfill behind the bricks with soil and tamp well as you secure the bricks in place. Install the patio surface material. Tap the tops of the bricks with a rubber mallet and a short 2 × 4 to level them with one another (inset).

Stone Edging

Cut stone or dressed stone makes better edging than flagstone, which often has jagged edges that create an uneven border. Semi-dressed stone, with one or more flat sides, is a good option for a more natural look.

Tools & Materials ▸

Rubber mallet
Maul
Stone chisel
Pitching chisel
Pointing chisel
Garden spade
Edging stones
Sand

Eye and ear
  protection
Work gloves
Mason's hammer
Shovel
Gravel base
Landscape fabric

Trimming Stone ▸

Trim irregular stones for a tight fit: first score a cutting line with a small stone chisel and maul, then complete the cut with a pitching chisel. Use a pointing chisel or the pick end of a mason's hammer to knock off small bumps and smooth rough edges.

Pitching chisel

How to Install Stone Edging

1

Excavate the patio or walkway site and dig a perimeter trench to accommodate the stone edging. Add the landscape fabric and then a gravel base, as required. Place each stone into the trench and tap it with a rubber mallet to set it into the gravel. Use your layout strings to keep the edging in line and at the proper height.

2

Backfill behind the stones with soil and tamp with a shovel handle or a board to secure the stones in the trench. If desired, fill the spaces between stones with sand or soil to help lock them together.

Concrete Curb Edging

Poured concrete edging is perfect for curves and custom shapes, especially when you want a continuous border at a consistent height. Keeping the edging low to the ground (about one inch above grade) makes it work well as a mowing strip, in addition to a patio or walkway border. Use fiber-reinforced concrete mix, and cut control joints into the edging to help control cracking.

Tools & Materials ▸

Rope or garden hose
Excavation tools
Mason's string
Hand tamp
Maul
Circular saw
Drill
Concrete mixing
  tools
Margin trowel
Wood concrete
  float

Concrete edger
1 × 1 wood stakes
¼" hardboard
1" wood screws
Fiber-reinforced
  concrete
Acrylic concrete
  sealer
Eye and ear
  protection
Work gloves

Concrete edging draws a sleek, smooth line between surfaces in your yard and is especially effective for curving paths and walkways.

How to Install Concrete Curb Edging

Lay out the contours of the edging using a rope or garden hose. For straight runs, use stakes and mason's string to mark the layout. Make the curb at least 5" wide.

Dig a trench between the layout lines 8" wide (or 3" wider than the finished curb width) at a depth that allows for a 4"-thick (minimum) curb at the desired height above grade. Compact the soil to form a flat, solid base.

Stake along the edges of the trench, using 1 × 1 × 12" wood stakes. Drive a stake every 18" along each side edge.

Build the form sides by fastening 4"-wide strips of ¼" hardboard to the insides of the stakes using 1" wood screws. Bend the strips to follow the desired contours.

Add spacers inside the form to maintain a consistent width. Cut the spacers from 1 × 1 to fit snugly inside the form. Set the spacers along the bottom edges of the form at 3-ft. intervals.

Fill the form with concrete mixed to a firm, workable consistency. Use a margin trowel to spread and consolidate the concrete.

Tool the concrete: once the bleed water disappears (see page 90), smooth the surface with a wood float. Using a margin trowel, cut 1"-deep control joints across the width of the curb at 3-ft. intervals. Tool the side edges of the curb with an edger. Allow to cure. Seal the concrete, as directed, with an acrylic concrete sealer, and let it cure for 3 to 5 days before removing the form.

Landscape Timber Edging

Pressure-treated landscape or cedar timbers make attractive, durable edging that's easy to install. Square-edged timbers are best for geometric pavers like brick and cut stone, while loose materials and natural flagstone look best with rounded or squared timbers. Choose the size of timber depending on how bold you want the border to look.

Tools & Materials ▸

Excavation tools
Plate compactor
  (available for rent)
Maul
Reciprocating saw
  with wood-cutting
  and metal-cutting
  blades, circular
  saw, or handsaw
Drill and ½" bit
Compacted gravel

Landscape fabric
Sand (optional)
Landscape timbers
  (pressure-treated
  or rot-resistant
  species only)
½"-diameter (#4)
  rebar
Eye and ear
  protection

Lumber or timber edging can be used with any patio surface material. Here, this lumber edging is not only decorative, it also holds all of the loose material in place.

How to Install Timber Edging

During the site excavation, dig a perimeter trench for the timbers so they will install flush with the top of the patio or walkway surface (or just above the surface for loose material). Add the compacted gravel base, as required, including a 2 to 4" layer in the perimeter trench. Cut timbers to the desired length using a reciprocating saw with a long wood-cutting blade, a circular saw, or a handsaw.

Drill ½" holes through each timber, close to the ends and every 24" in between. Cut a length of ½"-diameter (#4) rebar at 24" for each hole using a reciprocating saw and metal-cutting blade. Set the timbers in the trench and make sure they lie flat. Use your layout strings as guides for leveling and setting the height of the timbers. Anchor the timbers with the rebar, driving the bar flush with the wood surface.

Lumber Edging

Dimension lumber makes for an inexpensive edging material and a less-massive alternative to landscape timbers; 2 × 4 or 2 × 6 lumber works well for most patios and walkways. Use only pressure-treated lumber rated for ground contact or all-heart redwood or cedar boards to prevent rot. For the stakes, use pressure-treated lumber, since they will be buried anyway and appearance is not a concern.

Tools & Materials ▸

Excavation tools	Compacted gravel
Circular saw	Landscape fabric
Compactable gravel	Sand
Drill	2½" galvanized deck
2× lumber for edging	screws
2 × 4 lumber for	Eye and ear
stakes	protection
Wood preservative	

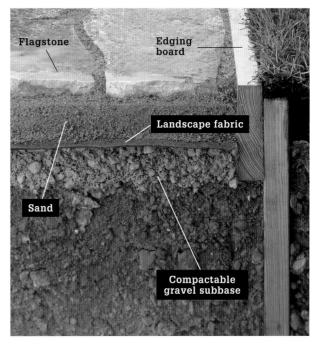

Wood edging is a popular choice for simple flagstone or paver walkways and for patios with a casual look.

How to Install Lumber Edging

Excavate the patio site, and dig a perimeter trench for the boards so they will install flush with the top of the patio surface (or just above the surface for loose material). Add the gravel base, as required, including a 2 to 4" layer of gravel in the trench. Cut the edging boards to length, and seal the ends with wood preservative. Cut 2 × 4 stakes about 16" long. Set the edging boards in the trench and drive a stake close to the ends of each board and every 24" in between.

Fasten the boards to the stakes with pairs of 2½" deck screws. Where boards meet at corners and butt joints, fasten them together with screws. Use your layout strings as guides for leveling and setting the height of the edging. Backfill behind the edging to support the boards and hide the stakes.

Sandset Brick Patio

Traditional clay brick pavers set in sand make for one of the simplest yet most rewarding patio projects. The installation process is straightforward and, because there's no mortar involved, you can complete the work at your own pace. The overall installation time depends on the patio's design.

Square-edged patios require fewer cuts and thus less time than curved designs. But if you want something out of the ordinary, sandset brick is a good material to work with—the small units are perfect for making curves and custom features; even if you have a lot of cuts, you can make them quickly and accurately with a rented masonry saw.

To pave with any of the classic patterns, such as running bond or herringbone, you'll start at one corner of your patio border or edging. To ensure accurate layout, check that the sides of the edging form a 90-degree angle at the starting corner. If you're not using edging or any kind of formal border, set up mason's strings to guide the brick placement.

If you go with clay brick without spacing lugs, use spacers cut from a sheet of ⅛"-thick hardboard to help set accurate sand-joint gaps as you lay the units.

Tools & Materials ▸

Tape measure	Professional-grade
Circular saw	landscape fabric
Drill	U-shaped wire
Excavation tools	stakes (optional)
Mason's string	Rigid paver edging
Stakes	1"-dia. pipe
Line level	Coarse sand
Plate compactor	Straight 2 × 4
(available for rent)	⅛" hardboard
Hand tamp	Plywood scrap
4-ft. level	Paver joint sand
Rubber mallet	Rake
Push broom	Trowel
Brick paver units	Masonry saw
Lumber (2 × 2,	Eye and ear
2 × 4)	protection
2½" drywall screws	Maul
Compactable gravel	Galvanized spikes
Work gloves	(for edging)

Brick pavers set in sand create a classic patio surface that's more casual than mortared pavers. The inherent flexibility of the sandset finish allows for easy repair and maintenance or changes in the design over time. It also creates good drainage.

How to Install a Sandset Brick Patio

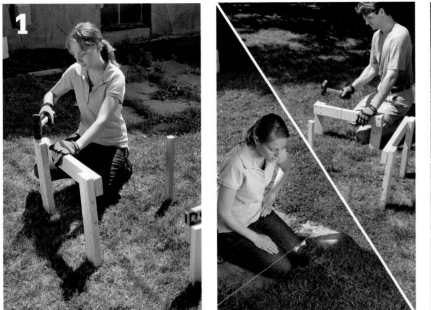

Set up batterboards and layout strings in a square or rectangle that's about 1 ft. larger than the excavation area (see pages 40 to 45 for detailed steps on layout and site preparation). Measure to make sure the string layout is square, and set the strings to follow a ⅛" per foot downward slope in the desired direction using a line level for guidance. Mark the excavation corners with stakes. The edges of the excavation should extend about 6" beyond the finished patio footprint.

Remove all sod and vegetation inside the area, reserving healthy sod for patching in around the finished patio.

Excavate the area to a depth that allows for a 6"-thick gravel subbase, a 1"-layer of sand, and the paver thickness; account for the desired height of the finished surface above the surrounding ground. Use cross strings and a story pole to check the depth as you work.

Add an even 3"-layer of compactable gravel over the entire site, and then tamp with a plate compactor. Repeat with another 3"-layer. The completed 6" gravel base prior to compacting must be smooth and flat, and it must follow the slope of the layout strings.

Install a layer of high-quality landscape fabric. Overlap rows of fabric by at least 6". If desired, pin the fabric in place with U-shaped wire stakes.

(continued)

Install rigid paver edging along two adjacent sides of the patio area, creating a perfect 90° corner. *Option: If you've laid out the pavers and taken precise measurements, you can install edging along three or four sides of the patio, as desired.* Trim the fabric along the back of the edging. Lay down lengths of 1"-dia. pipe in parallel lines about 3 to 6 ft. apart.

Add a 1"-thick layer of coarse sand. Smooth it out with a rake so it just covers the pipes. Dampen the sand with water, then pack it down lightly with a hand tamp.

Screed the sand perfectly flat using a straight, long 2 × 4: rest the board on top of the pipes, and pull it backward with a side-to-side sawing motion. Fill in low spots with sand as you work. Dampen, tamp, and screed the sand again until the surface is smooth and flat and firmly packed. Remove the pipe(s) in the area where you will begin the paving.

Fill the depression left by the pipe with sand, and then smooth it out with a short board or a trowel. Tamp the area with the hand tamp, and smooth again as needed so the filled-in area is perfectly flat. *Note: Repeat this step as needed during the paving process.*

10

Begin setting the border bricks, starting at the right-angle corner of the patio edging, using ⅛" hardboard spacers if necessary. Complete the border row that will be parallel to the first course of field brick, and continue several feet up the perpendicular side edge. For gentle curves, use full bricks set with slightly angled (wedge-shaped) sand joints; tighter curves require cut bricks for a good fit.

11

Field units

Border units

Set the first course of field brick. These bricks should be centered over the sand joints of the completed border row. Use a mason's string tied between two bricks to align the leading edges of the first-course bricks. After setting several bricks, tap them with a rubber mallet to bed them into the sand layer. Complete the first field course, and then add some border units along the edge.

12

Snug a piece of edging against the installed brick and anchor it in place. Note: Install the remaining edging as the paving progresses. Continue setting the brick using the mason's string and spacers for consistent spacing and alignment.

Cutting Pavers & Bricks ▸

If your design requires cuts, use a masonry saw (tub saw). These water-lubricated cutting tools are available for rent at most building centers and stone yards.

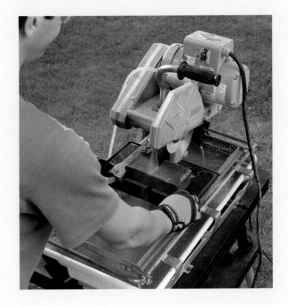

(continued)

13

Check each 4-ft. section for level to make sure the bricks are even across the top. Remove low or high bricks and add or remove sand beneath to bring them flush with the surrounding bricks. Work atop a plywood platform to prevent displacing the bricks. Complete the paving.

Variation: If your patio design includes curves or rounded corners, mark bricks for cutting curves by holding each brick in position and marking the desired cutting line onto the top face, then make the cuts with a masonry saw. For complex curves, it might be easier to leave off the border bricks and run the field brick long at the edges, then mark the curved cuts onto the field brick (see page 148).

14

15

16

Spread sand over the surface, then sweep the sand to fill the joints. Sweep the surface clean, and then tamp the surface with the plate compactor to settle the sand in the joints and lock the bricks in place.

Fill and tamp the sand joints one or more times until the joints are completely filled after compaction. Sweep up any loose sand.

Soak the surface with water and let it dry. If necessary, fill and tamp again, then hose off the surface and let it dry.

90° herringbone patterns require bricks that are twice as long as they are wide. Start the pattern with two bricks set in the corner of your edging (edging must form a precise 90° angle). Add half-bricks next to the ends of the first two bricks. Complete the next row, zigzagging full bricks following the first row. Repeat the zigzag pattern for the remaining field bricks, adding half-bricks at the ends of rows as needed.

45° herringbone patterns require bricks that are twice as long as they are wide. Starting from a precise 90° corner, set the first row with two right-angle half-bricks. Complete the second row with two right-angle half-bricks flanking a full brick. Begin each remaining field row zig-zagging full bricks and finishing with right-angle half-bricks or trimmed bricks beveled at 45°.

Basketweave patterns require bricks that are twice as long as they are wide. To avoid cuts (on square or rectangular patios), you can install edging on only one side and use it as a baseline for the paving. Install the remaining three sides of edging after all bricks are laid. Snap a chalk line down the center of the sand bed, making sure it is perpendicular (90°) to the baseline edging. Working from the centerline out for each section, lay bricks in a pyramid shape, setting 12 bricks total in the first row, 8 in the second row, and 4 in the third row. Complete the paving by adding to each row incrementally to maintain the pyramid shape. This ensures that every row stems from the centerline to keep the layout straight.

Pinwheels allow you to avoid cuts (on square or rectangular patios) by installing edging on only two adjacent sides, starting from a precise 90° corner. Install the remaining edging after the paving is complete. Set each square pattern using four full bricks, as shown here, then fill the center cavity with a half-brick. For added accent, the centerpiece can be a unique color, but it must be the same thickness as the full bricks. Do not use a thinner brick for the center and compensate for the difference with additional sand; the brick will eventually sink and create an uneven surface.

Walkways & Steps

A walkway or path can do much more than provide a route for foot traffic. A path can be a versatile design element, creating an attractive border along a house, a patio, or landscape features. It can also become an attractive transition between two areas, such as a lawn and a planting bed.

Walkways and paths are also effective at unifying spaces in the landscape. For example, imagine a back yard with a patio at one end, a beautiful flower garden at the other, and a solid swath of lawn in-between. By adding a footpath, you connect all of the areas.

In terms of construction techniques and material, a walkway is essentially a patio in a different configuration. All of the same materials that make great patio surfaces are equally as suitable for walkways. In this chapter, you'll find complete projects utilizing all major walkway materials, plus some you might not have thought of. As in the chapter on patio projects, there's also a special section with tips for planning your walkway project and laying out the site (see pages 140 to 143).

In this chapter:

Designing & Laying Out Walkways & Steps

Designing and planning a new walkway starts with a careful assessment of how the path will be used. Landscape designers commonly group outdoor walkways into three main categories, according to use and overall design goals.

The first is a *primary walkway*: a high-traffic path used by household members and visitors, such as a walkway between the street and the home's main entry door. A main path should provide the quickest and easiest route from point A to point B. Any unnecessary twists and turns are likely to be cross-cut by walkers, leaving you with a less manicured path through the yard. To allow two people to walk side-by-side, a main path should be 42 to 48 inches wide. Surface materials should be durable, slip-resistant, and easy to shovel (if you live in a snowy climate), such as poured concrete, pavers, or flat stones.

A *secondary walkway* typically connects the house to a patio or outbuilding or a patio to a well-used area in the yard. A comfortable width for single-person travel is 24 to 36 inches. Surfaces should be flat and level underfoot and provide good drainage and slip-resistance in all seasons.

The third type, a *tertiary path*, is informal, perhaps nothing more than a line of stepping stones meandering through a flower garden or a simple gravel path leading to a secluded seating area. Design tertiary paths for a comfortable stride, with a minimum width of 12 to 16 inches.

Once you've established the design criteria for your walkway or path, spend some time testing the size and configuration of the route to be sure it will meet your needs. See page 143 for help with planning a set of stairs for your walkway or landscape.

As an important part of a home's curb appeal, a primary walkway should be styled to complement the house exterior and street-side landscaping.

Secondary walkways can be a blend of practicality and decoration. A gentle curve here and there adds interest without slowing travel too much.

A tertiary path can be as rustic or creative as you like. It can serve as an invitation to stroll through a garden or an access path for tending plants—or both.

Tools & Materials ›

Stakes	Lumber (1 × 2,
Mason's string	1 × 4, 2 × 4)
Maul	Level
Plate compactor	Drill and drill bit
Compactable gravel	Cardboard
Excavation tools	Screws
Line level	Eye and ear
¾" rope	protection
Marking paint	Work gloves

How to Lay Out a Straight Walkway

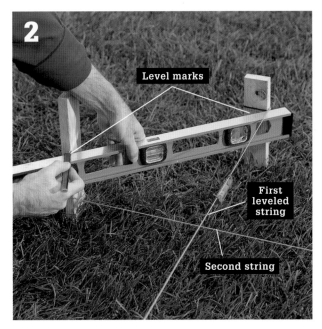

Use temporary stakes and mason's string to plan the walkway layout. Drive stakes at the ends of each section and at any corners, then tie the strings to the stakes to represent the edges of the finished path. Run a second set of strings 6" outside the first lines.

Set up a new string layout to mark the precise borders of the finished walkway. Along the high edge of the walkway, set the strings to the finished surface height. Use a line level to make sure the strings are level. *Tip: For 90° turns, use the 3-4-5 technique to set the strings accurately at 90° (see page 43).*

Set the border strings lower for the slope. The finished surface follows a downward slope of ¼" per foot on the opposite side of the walkway. Use a homemade slope gauge to set the height of the strings (see step 3, page 142). Fine-tune the gravel base to follow the slope setting, and prepare for the sand bed and/or surface material.

Excavate the area within the string lines. First, cut sod along the inside edge of the second string line. Remove all grass and plantings from the excavation area. Add the gravel subbase.

How to Lay Out Curving or Irregular Walkways

Experiment with different sizes and shapes for the walkway using two lengths of ¾" braided rope or a garden hose. To maintain a consistent width, cut spacers from 1 × 2 lumber and use them to set the spacing between the rope outlines.

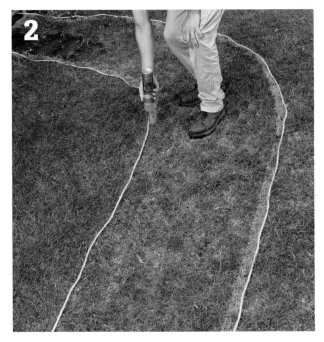

Mark the ground with marking paint, following the final outline of the ropes. Excavate the area 6" beyond the marked outline (or as required for your choice of edging, see pages 124 to 131). If desired, you can set up a string layout to guide the installation of the gravel subbase (see page 141).

Create a slope gauge for checking the slope of your gravel base, edging, or surface material. Tape a level and a drill bit to a straight 2 × 4 that's a little longer than the width of the walkway. The slope should be ¼" per foot: for a 2-ft. level, use a ½"-dia. bit or spacer; for a 4-ft. level, use a 1"-thick spacer. The slope is correct when the level reads level.

Planning a Stepping Stone Path ▸

To plan a simple stepping stone path, cut pieces of cardboard to roughly the same size as an average stone you're using. Lay out the pieces in the desired route, then walk along the "stones" to make sure the spacing is comfortable for walking with a casual stride. Leave the test pieces in place to guide the excavation and/or stone setting.

How to Plan Landscape Steps

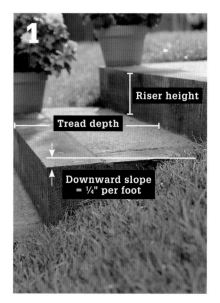

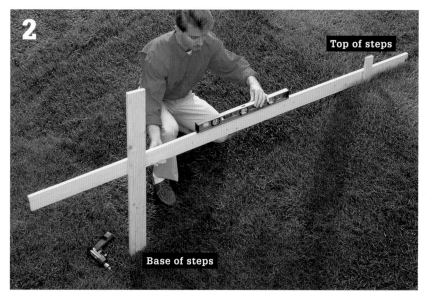

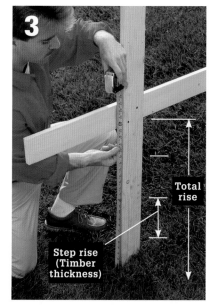

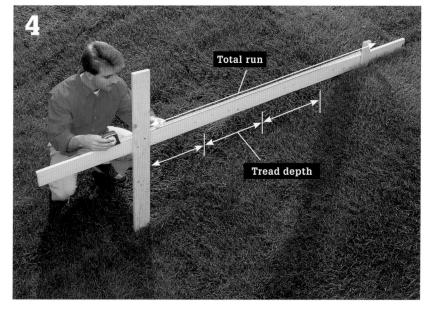

Landscape steps are best with a riser height (vertical dimension) of 6" or less and a tread depth (horizontal dimension) of 11" or more. Plan to build each tread with a downward slope of ¼" per foot from back to front. Complete the following steps to calculate the tread and riser dimensions for your steps.

Drive a tall stake into the ground at the base of the stairway site. Adjust the stake so it is perfectly plumb. Drive a shorter stake at the top of the site. Position a long, straight 1 × 4 or 2 × 4 against the stakes, with one end touching the ground next to the top stake. Adjust the 1 × 4 so it is level, then attach it to the stakes with screws. For long spans, use a mason's string instead of a board.

Measure from the ground to the bottom of the 1 × 4 to find the total rise of the stairway. Divide the total rise by the desired riser height to find the number of steps you need. If the result contains a fraction, drop the fraction and divide the rise by the whole number to find the exact riser dimension.

Measure along the 1 × 4 between the stakes to find the total horizontal run of the stairway. Divide the total run by the number of steps to find the depth of each step tread. If the depth is less than 11", revise the step layout to extend the depth of the treads.

Sandset Brick Walkway

Sandset brick is a good choice of material for a walkway for the same reasons that make it a great patio surface—it's easy to work with, it lends itself equally well to traditional paving patterns and creative custom designs, and it can be installed at a leisurely pace because there's no mortar or wet concrete involved. The timeless look of natural clay brick is especially well-suited to walkways, where the rhythmic patterns of geometric lines create a unique sense of movement that draws your eye down the path toward its destination.

In this walkway project, all of the interior (*field*) bricks are arranged in the installation area and then the curving side edges of the walk are marked onto the set bricks to ensure perfect cutting lines. After the edge bricks are cut and reset, border bricks are installed followed by rigid paver edging to keep everything in place. This is the most efficient method for installing a curving path. Straight walkways can follow the standard process of installing the edging and border bricks (on one or both sides of the path, as applicable) before laying the field brick, as is done in the brick patio project.

With standard brick, you'll need to set the gaps with spacers cut from ⅛" hardboard, as shown in this project.

Tools & Materials ▸

Tape measure	Coarse sand
¾" braided rope	Landscape fabric
Marking paint	Landscape staples
Excavation tools	Brick paver units
Plate compactor	Plastic patio edging
Mason's string	⅛" hardboard
Stakes	Paver joint sand
Hand tamp	Eye and ear
2- or 4-ft. level	protection
Drill bits	Work gloves
Rubber mallet	12" galvanized
Straightedge	spikes
Trowel	Maul
Masonry saw	
Push broom	
1 × 2 lumber	
Compactable gravel	
Straight 2 × 4	
Duct tape	

A curving brick walkway can be as much a design statement as a course for easy travel. Curves require more time than straight designs, due to the extra cutting involved, but the results can be all the more stunning.

How to Install a Sandset Brick Walkway

Lay out the walkway curved edges using ¾" braided rope (or use mason's strings for straight sections; shown as variation). Cut 1 × 2 or 2 × 2 spacers to the desired path width and then place them in-between the ropes for consistent spacing. Mark the outlines along the inside edges of the ropes onto the ground with marking paint.

Excavate the area 6" outside of the marked lines along both sides of the path. Remove soil to allow for a 4"-thick subbase of gravel, a 1" layer of sand, and the thickness of the brick pavers (minus the height of the finished paving above the ground). The finished paving typically rests about 1" aboveground for ease of lawn maintenance. Thoroughly tamp the area with a plate compactor.

Spread out an even layer of compactable gravel— enough for a 4"-thick layer after compaction. Grade the gravel to follow a downward slope of ¼" per foot (most long walkways slope from side to side, while shorter paths or walkway sections can be sloped along their length). Use a homemade slope gauge to screed the gravel smooth and to check the slope as you work (see step 3, page 142). Tamp the subbase thoroughly with the plate compactor, making sure the surface is flat and smooth and properly sloped.

(continued)

Cover the gravel base with professional-grade landscape fabric, overlapping the strips by at least 6". If desired, tack the fabric in place with landscape staples.

Spread a 1"-layer of coarse sand over the landscape fabric. Screed the sand with a board so it is smooth, even, and flat.

Tamp the screeded sand with a hand tamper or a plate compactor. Check the slope of the surface as you go.

Spacer

Begin the paving at one end of the walkway, following the desired pattern. Use ⅛"-thick hardboard spacers in-between the bricks to set the sand-joint gaps. *Tip: It's best to start the paving against a straightedge or square corner. If your walkway does not connect to a patio or stoop, set a temporary 2 × 4 with stakes at the end of the walkway to create a straight starting line.*

Spacer

Option: If your walkway includes long straight sections between curves, set up guidelines with stakes and mason's strings to keep the ends of the courses straight as you pave.

8

Spacer

Set the next few courses of brick, running them long over the side edges. With the first few courses in place, tap the bricks with a rubber mallet to bed them into the sand.

9

Lay out the curved edges of the finished walkway using ¾" braided rope . Adjust the ropes as needed so that the cut bricks will be roughly symmetrical on both edges of the walkway. Also measure between the ropes to make sure the finished width will be accurate according to your layout. Trace along the ropes with a pencil to mark the cutting lines onto the bricks.

(continued)

Variation: Cut field bricks after installing the edging. Mark each brick for cutting by hlding it in position and drawing the cut line across the top face.

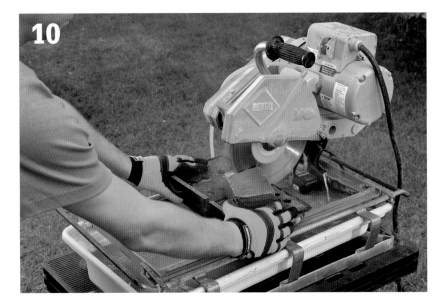

Cut the bricks with a rented masonry saw (wet saw), following the instructions from the tool supplier. Make straight cuts with a single, full-depth cut. Curved cuts require multiple straight cuts made tangentially to the cutting line. After cutting a brick, reset it before cutting the next brick.

Align the border bricks (if applicable) snug against the edges of the field paving. Use a straightedge or level to make sure the border units are flush with the tops of the field bricks. Set the border bricks with a rubber mallet. Dampen the exposed edges of the sand bed, and then use a trowel to slice away the edge so it's flush with the paving.

Install rigid paver edging (bendable) (see page 125) or other edge material tight against the outside of the walkway.

Fill and tamp the sand joints one or more times until the joints are completely filled. Sweep up any loose sand (see page 136).

Soak the surface with water and let it dry. Cover the edging sides with soil and sod or other material, as desired.

Poured Concrete Walkway

If you've always wanted to try your hand at creating with concrete, an outdoor walkway is a great project to start with. The basic elements and construction steps of a walkway are similar to those of a poured concrete patio or other landscape slab, but the smaller scale of a walkway makes it a much more manageable project for first-timers. Placing the wet concrete goes faster, and you can easily reach the center of the surface for finishing from either side of the walkway.

Like a patio slab, a poured concrete walkway also makes a good foundation for mortared surface materials, like pavers, stone, and tile. If that's your goal, be sure to account for the thickness of the surface material when planning and laying out the walkway height. A coarse broomed or scratched finish on the concrete will help create a strong bond with the mortar bed of the surface material.

The walkway in this project is a 4-inch-thick by 26"-wide concrete slab with a broom finish for slip resistance. It consists of two straight, 12-ft.-long runs connected by a 90° elbow. After curing, the walkway can be left bare for a classic, low-maintenance surface, or it can be colored with a permanent acid stain (see pages 96 to 97). When planning your walkway project, consult your city's building department for recommendations and construction requirements.

Tools & Materials ▸

Drill, bits	7⁄16" hardboard siding
Circular saw	Compactable gravel
Mason's string	6 × 6" 10/10 welded
Line level	wire mesh (wwm)
Excavation tools	Tie wire
2- or 4-ft. level	2" bolsters
Plate compactor	Isolation board
Heavy-duty wire	and construction
cutters or bolt	adhesive
cutters	Release agent
Concrete mixing	4,000 psi concrete
tools	(or as required by
Shovel	local code)
Hammer	Clear polyethylene
Magnesium float	sheeting
Edger tool	Eye and ear
Groover tool	protection
Magnesium trowel	Work gloves
Push broom	4" deck screws
Lumber (2 × 2,	#3 rebar (optional)
2 × 4)	Wood stakes
Drywall screws	Tape measure
(2½", 3½")	

Poured concrete walkways can be designed with straight lines, curves, or any angles you desire. The flat, hardwearing surface is ideal for frequently traveled paths and will stand up to heavy equipment and decades of snow shoveling.

Sloping a Walkway

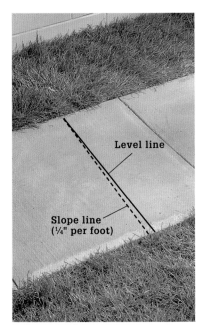

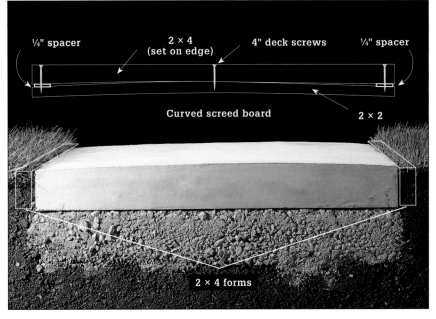

Straight slope: Set the concrete form lower on one side of the walkway so the finished surface is flat and slopes downward at a rate of ¼" per foot. Always slope the surface away from the house foundation or, when not near the house, toward the area best suited to accept water runoff.

Crowned slope: When a walkway does not run near the house foundation, you have the option of crowning the surface so it slopes down to both sides. To make the crown, construct a curved screed board by cutting a 2 × 2 and a 2 × 4 long enough to rest on both sides of the concrete form. Sandwich the boards together with a ¼"-thick spacer at each end, then fasten the assembly with 4" deck screws driven at the center and the ends. Use the board to screed the concrete (see step 8, page 154).

Reinforcing a Walkway

As an alternative to the wire mesh reinforcement used in the following project, you can reinforce a walkway slab with metal rebar (check with the local building code requirements). For a 3-ft.-wide walkway, lay two sections of #3 rebar spaced evenly inside the concrete form. Bend the rebar as needed to follow curves or angles. Overlap pieces by 12" and tie them together with tie wire. Use wire bolsters to suspend the bar in the middle of the slab's thickness.

How to Install a Poured Concrete Walkway

Lay out the precise edges of the finished walkway using stakes (or batterboards) and mason's string (see pages 40 to 45 for additional help with setting up and using layout strings). Where possible, set stakes 12" or so outside of the walkway edges so they're out of the way. Make sure any 90° corners are square using the 3-4-5 measuring technique. Level the strings, then lower the strings on one side of the layout to create a downward slope of ¼" per foot (if the walkway will be crowned instead of sloped to one side, keep all strings level with one another. Cut away the sod or other plantings 6" beyond the layout lines on all sides of the site.

Excavate the site for a 4- to 6"-thick gravel subbase, plus any subgrade (below ground level) portion of the slab, as desired. Measure the depth with a story pole (see page 43) against the high-side layout strings, then use a slope gauge (see page 142) to grade the slope. Tamp the soil thoroughly with a plate compactor.

Cover the site with a 4- to 6"-layer of gravel and screed the surface flat, checking with a slope gauge to set the proper grade. Compact the gravel so the top surface is 4" below the finished walkway height. Reset the layout strings at the precise height of the finished walkway.

Build the concrete form with straight 2 × 4 lumber so the inside faces of the form are aligned with the strings. Drive 2 × 4 stakes for reinforcement behind butt joints. Align the form with the layout strings, and then drive stakes at each corner and every 2 to 3 ft. in-between. Fasten the form to the stakes so the top inside corner of the form boards are just touching the layout strings. The tops of the stakes should be just below the tops of the form.

Add curved strips made from ¼- to ⅜"-thick plywood hardboard or lauan to create curved corners, if desired. Secure curved strips by screwing them to wood stakes. Recheck the gravel bed inside the concrete form, making sure it is smooth and properly sloped.

Lay reinforcing wire mesh over the gravel base, keeping the edges 1 to 2" from the insides of the form. Overlap the mesh strips by 6" (one square) and tie them together with tie wire. Prop up the mesh on 2" bolsters placed every few feet and tied to the mesh with wire. Install isolation board (see page 98) where the walkway adjoins other slabs or structures. When you're ready for the concrete pour, coat the insides of the form with a release agent or vegetable oil.

Drop the concrete in pods, starting at the far end of the walkway. Distribute it around the form by placing it (don't throw it) with a shovel. As you fill, stab into the concrete with the shovel, and tap a hammer against the back sides of the form to eliminate air pockets. Continue until the form is evenly filled, slightly above the tops of the form.

(continued)

8

Immediately screed the surface with a straight 2 × 4: two people pull the board backward in a side-to-side sawing motion with the board resting on top of the form. As you work, shovel in extra concrete to fill low spots or remove concrete from high spots, and re-screed. The goal is to create a flat surface that's level with the top of the form.

9

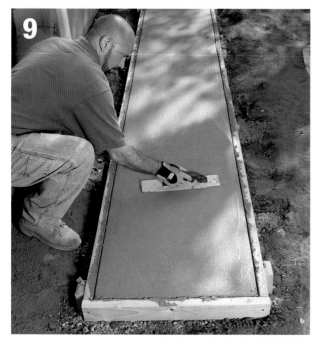

Float the concrete surface with a magnesium float, working back and forth in broad arching strokes. Tip up the leading edge of the tool slightly to prevent gouging the surface. Stop floating once the surface is relatively smooth and has a wet sheen. Be careful not to over-float, indicated by water pooling on the surface. Allow the bleed water to disappear and the concrete to harden sufficiently (see page 90).

10

Use an edger to shape the side edges of the walkway along the wood form. Carefully run the edger back and forth along the form to create a smooth, rounded corner, lifting the leading edge of the tool slightly to prevent gouging.

Mark the locations of the control joints onto the top edges of the form boards, spacing the joints at intervals 1½ times the width of the walkway.

Cut the control joints with a 1" groover guided by a straight 2 × 4 held (or fastened) across the form at the marked locations. Make several light passes back and forth until the groove reaches full depth, lifting the leading edge of the tool to prevent gouging. Remove the guide board once each joint is complete. If desired, smooth out the marks made by the groover using a magnesium trowel.

Create a nonslip surface with a broom finish: starting at the far side edge of the walkway, steadily drag a broom backward over the surface in a straight line using a single pulling motion. Repeat in single, parallel passes (with minimal or no overlap), and rinse off the broom bristles after each pass. The stiffer and coarser the broom, the rougher the texture will be.

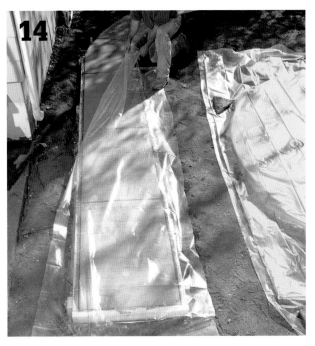

Cure the concrete by misting the walkway with water, then covering it with clear polyethylene sheeting. Smooth out any air pockets (which can cause discoloration), and weight down the sheeting along the edges. Mist the surface and reapply the plastic daily for 1 to 2 weeks.

Decorative Concrete Path

A well-made walkway or garden path not only stands up to years of hard use, it enhances the natural landscape and complements a home's exterior features. While traditional walkway materials like brick and stone have always been prized for both appearance and durability, most varieties are quite pricey and often difficult to install. As an easy and inexpensive alternative, you can build a new concrete path using manufactured forms. The result is a beautiful pathway that combines the custom look of brick or natural stone with all the durability and economy of poured concrete.

Building a path is a great do-it-yourself project. Once you've laid out the path, you mix the concrete, set and fill the form, then lift off the form to reveal the finished design. After a little troweling to smooth the surfaces, you're ready to create the next section—using the same form. Simply repeat the process until the path is complete. Each form creates a section that's approximately two square feet using one 80-lb. bag of premixed concrete. This project shows you all the basic steps for making any length of pathway, plus special techniques for making curves, adding a custom finish, or coloring the concrete to suit your personal design.

Tools & Materials ▸

Excavation and site preparation tools
Concrete mold
Wheelbarrow or mixing box
Shovel
Margin trowel or concrete finishing trowel
Fiber-reinforced concrete mix
Work gloves
Liquid concrete colorant
Clear polyethylene sheeting
Polymer-modified jointing sand or mortar mix
Compactable gravel (optional)
Level
Broom or stiff brush

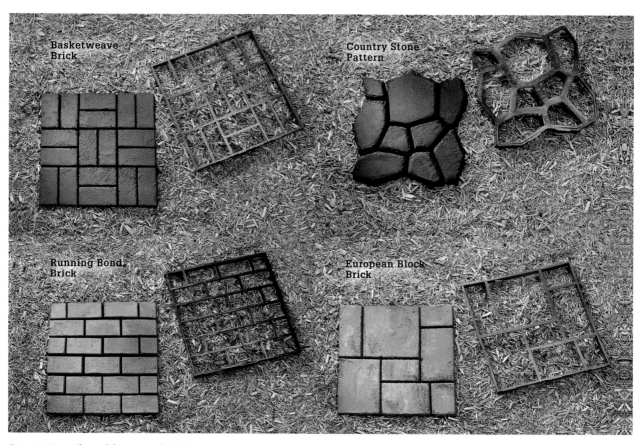

Concrete path molds are available in a range of styles and decorative patterns. Coloring the wet concrete is a great way to add a realistic look to the path design.

How to Create a Straight or 90° Decorative Concrete Path

Prepare the project site by leveling the ground, removing sod or soil as needed. For a more durable base, excavate the area and add 2 to 4" of compactable gravel. Grade and compact the gravel layer so it is level and flat. See pages 140 to 143 for detailed steps on layout and site preparation.

Mix a batch of concrete for the first section, following the product directions (see page 158 to add color, as we have done here). Place the form at the start of your path and level it, if desired. Shovel the wet concrete into the form to fill each cavity. Consolidate and smooth the surface of the form using a concrete margin trowel.

Promptly remove the form, and then trowel the edges of the section to create the desired finish (it may help to wet the trowel in water). For a nonslip surface, broom the section or brush it with a stiff brush. Place the form against the finished section and repeat steps 2 and 3 to complete the next section.

After removing each form, remember to trowel the edges of the section to create the desired finish. Repeat until the path is finished. If desired, rotate the form 90° with each section to vary the pattern. Cure the path by covering it with polyethylene sheeting for 5 to 7 days, lifting the plastic and misting the concrete with water each day.

(continued)

5

Fill walkway joints with sand or mortar mix to mimic the look of hand-laid stone or brick. Sweep the sand or dry mortar into the section contours and spaces between sections. For mortar, mist the joints with water so they harden in place.

Custom Surfacing Tip ▸

Create custom surface finishes by pressing small stones or pea gravel into the wet concrete or by brushing on a layer of sand. Apply finish materials after the concrete has reached its initial set (thumb print hard) but is still damp—approximately one hour after placing.

Coloring Your Concrete ▸

Adding colorant to the concrete mix is the easiest method and produces consistent results:

1. Combine liquid concrete colorant with water and mix into each bag-quantity of dry concrete mix, following the manufacturer's instructions. Blend thoroughly for consistent coloring, then add clean water to the mix, as needed, to achieve the proper consistency for pouring the concrete.

2. After placing and finishing the path sections, cure the concrete carefully to produce the best color quality. If curing conditions will be less than ideal, apply concrete sealer to ensure slow, even curing and good coloring.

Coloring gives molded concrete a more natural-looking finish and is great for blending your path or walkway into your landscape design.

How to Create a Curved Decorative Concrete Path

After removing the form from a freshly poured section (see page 157, steps 1 through 3), reposition the form in the direction of the curve and press down to slice off the inside corner of the section (photo left). Trowel the cut edge (and the rest of the section) to finish. Pour the next section following the curve (photo right). Cut off as many sections as needed to complete the curve. Cure the path by covering it with plastic sheeting for 5 to 7 days, lifting the plastic and misting the concrete with water each day.

Sprinkle the area around the joint or joints between pavers with polymer-modified jointing sand after the concrete has cured sufficiently so that the sand does not adhere. Sweep the product into the gap to clean the paver surfaces while filling the gap.

Mist the jointing sand with clean water, taking care not to wash the sand out of the joint. Once the water dries, the polymers in the mixture will have hardened the sand to look like a mortar joint. Refresh as needed.

Mortared Brick Over a Concrete Path

If you're looking to makeover an aging concrete walkway, you can't beat the looks and performance of mortared brick paving. The flat, finished surface is ideal for both heavy foot traffic and garden equipment and is nearly as maintenance-free as plain concrete, while the formal elegance of brick is a dramatic upgrade over a timeworn, gray slab. If your plans include new paving over an old concrete patio, a walkway is also the perfect opportunity to develop your skills before tackling the larger patio surface—the materials and techniques are the same for both applications.

Start your walkway project with a careful examination of the concrete path: as the structural foundation of your new surface, the concrete must be stable and relatively flat. Large cracks and uneven surfaces indicate movement of the concrete structure, often due to problems with the gravel base and/or inadequate drainage under the slab. Since these ailments won't go away with the new paving, you can either decide to replace the old concrete with a newly poured walkway or consider a mortarless surface, such as sandset brick. With that in mind, minor surface problems, such as fine cracks and cosmetic flaws, will not likely affect new mortared paving.

When shopping for pavers, consider the added height of the new surface, the paving pattern you desire, and the material of the pavers themselves. Natural clay brick pavers are available in standard (approximately 2⅜") and thinner (approximately 1½") thicknesses. Concrete pavers are installed using the same techniques, and they come in a range of sizes, thicknesses, and shapes. In any case, be sure to choose straight-sided pavers, as irregular or interlocking shapes make for unnecessarily tricky mortar work. Consult with knowledgeable staff at your masonry supplier to learn about paver materials and mortar suitable for your project and the local climate.

Tools & Materials ▸

Shovel	Brick or concrete
Mortar mixing tools	pavers
Mason's trowel	½" plywood
V-shaped mortar tool	Straight 2 × 4
(jointing tool)	or 2 × 6
Rubber mallet	Coarse rag
4-ft. level	Clear polyethylene
Mortar bag	sheeting
Type S mortar (or	Eye and ear
other recom-	protection
mended type)	

The natural, warm color of brick is a dramatic yet DIY-friendly upgrade for a tired looking gray slab.

How to Install Mortared Brick over a Concrete Path

Dig a trench around the concrete path, slightly wider than the thickness of one paver. Dig the trench so it is about 3½" below the concrete surface (for standard-sized pavers).

Sweep the old concrete, then hose off the surface and sides with water to clear away dirt and debris. Soak the pavers with water before mortaring; dry pavers absorb moisture, weakening the mortar strength. Mix a small batch of mortar according to manufacturer's directions. For convenience, place the mortar on a scrap of plywood.

Install edging bricks by applying a ½"-layer of mortar to the side of the concrete slab and to one side of each brick. Set bricks into the trench, against the concrete. Brick edging should be ½" higher than the thickness of the brick pavers.

Finish the joints on the edging bricks with a V-shaped mortar tool, then mix and apply a ½"-thick bed of mortar to one end of the sidewalk using a trowel. Mortar hardens very quickly, so work in sections no larger than 4 sq. ft.

(continued)

Make a screed board for smoothing the mortar by notching the ends of a straight 2 × 4 or 2 × 6 to fit between the edging bricks. The depth of the notches should equal the thickness of the pavers. Drag the screed across the mortar bed until the mortar is smooth.

Lay the paving bricks one at a time into the mortar, maintaining a ½" gap between pavers. (A piece of scrap plywood works well as a spacing guide.) Set the pavers by tapping them lightly with a rubber mallet.

As each section of pavers is completed, check with a straightedge or level to make sure the tops of the pavers are even. If a paver is too high, press it down or tap it with the rubber mallet; if too low, lift it out and butter its back face with mortar and reset it.

When all the pavers are installed, use a mortar bag to fill the joints between the pavers with fresh mortar. Work in 4-sq.-ft. sections, and avoid getting mortar on the tops of the pavers.

Use a V-shaped mortar tool to finish the joints as you complete each 4 sq.-ft. section. For best results, finish the longer joints first, then the shorter joints. Use a trowel to remove excess mortar.

Let the mortar dry for a few hours, then scrub the pavers with a coarse rag and water. Cover the walkway with polyethylene sheeting and let the mortar cure for at least 24 hours. Remove sheeting, but do not walk on the pavers for at least three days.

Variation: As an alternative to paving over an entire walkway (if the old concrete still looks good), add a decorative touch with a border of mortared pavers along the edges. The same treatment is great for dressing up the exposed edges of a concrete patio, stoop, or steps. To install edging along a walkway, follow the basic techniques shown in steps 1 to 4 on page 161, but set the pavers flush with the walkway surface. Position the pavers horizontally or vertically, depending on the height of the walkway and the desired effect. After the pavers are set and tooled, follow step 10 above to complete the job.

Flagstone Walkway

Natural flagstone is an ideal material for creating landscape floors. It's attractive and durable and blends well with both formal and informal landscapes. Although flagstone structures are often mortared, they can also be constructed with the sand-set method. Sand-setting flagstones is much faster and easier than setting them with mortar.

There are a variety of flat, thin sedimentary rocks that can be used for this project. Home and garden stores often carry several types of flagstone, but stone supply yards usually have a greater variety. Some varieties of flagstone cost more than others, but there are many affordable options. When you buy the flagstone for your project, select pieces in a variety of sizes from large to small. Arranging the stones for your walkway is similar to putting together a puzzle, and you'll need to see all the pieces laid out.

The following example demonstrates how to build a straight flagstone walkway with wood edging. If you'd like to build a curved walkway, select another edging material, such as brick or cut stone. Instead of filling gaps between stones with sand, you might want to fill them with topsoil and plant grass or some other ground cover between the stones. See pages 140 to 143 for help with designing a walkway and preparing the project site.

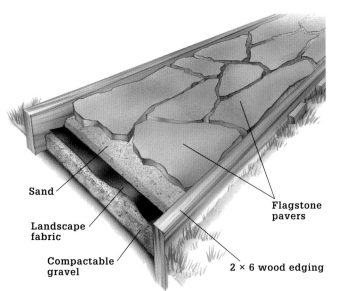

Sand

Landscape fabric

Compactable gravel

Flagstone pavers

2 × 6 wood edging

Tools & Materials ▸

Excavation tools
Circular saw with
  masonry blade
Power drill
Masonry chisel
Maul
Rubber mallet
Landscape fabric
Sand

2 × 6 pressure-
  treated lumber
Deck screws
Compactable gravel
Flagstone pavers
Eye and ear
  protection
Work gloves

Flagstone walkways combine durability with beauty and work well for casual or formal landscapes.

How to Build a Flagstone Walkway

Lay out, excavate, and prepare the base for the walkway. Form edging by installing 2 × 6 pressure-treated lumber around the perimeter of the pathway. Drive stakes on the outside of the edging, spaced 12" apart. The tops of the stakes should be below ground level. Drive galvanized screws through the edging and into the stakes.

Test-fit the stones over the walkway base, finding an attractive arrangement that limits the number of cuts needed. The gaps between the stones should range between ⅜ and 2" wide. Use a pencil to mark the stones for cutting, then remove the stones and place them beside the walkway in the same arrangement. Score along the marked lines with a circular saw and masonry blade set to ⅛" blade depth. Set a piece of wood under the stone, just inside the scored line. Use a masonry chisel and maul to strike along the scored line until the stone breaks.

Lay overlapping strips of landscape fabric over the walkway base and spread a 2"-layer of sand over it. Make a screed board from a short 2 × 6, notched to fit inside the edging. Pull the screed from one end of the walkway to the other, adding sand as needed to create a level base.

Beginning at one corner of the walkway, lay the flagstones onto the sand base. Repeat the arrangement you created in step 2, with ⅜- to 2"-wide gaps between stones. If necessary, add or remove sand to level the stones, then set them by tapping them with a rubber mallet or a length of 2 × 4.

Fill the gaps between the stones with sand. (Use topsoil, if you're going to plant grass or ground cover between the stones.) Pack sand into the gaps, then spray the entire walkway with water to help settle the sand. Repeat until the gaps are completely filled and tightly packed with sand.

Loose materials can be used as filler between solid surface materials, like flagstone, or laid as the primary ground cover, as shown here.

Simple Gravel Path

Loose-fill gravel pathways are perfect for stone gardens, casual yards, and other situations where a hard surface is not required. The material is inexpensive, and its fluidity accommodates curves and irregular edging. Since gravel may be made from any rock, gravel paths may be matched to larger stones in the environment, tying them in to your landscaping. The gravel you choose need not be restricted to stone, either. Industrial and agricultural byproducts, such as cinder and ashes, walnut shells, seashells, and ceramic fragments may also be used as path material.

For a more stable path, choose angular or jagged gravel over rounded materials. However, if your preference is to stroll throughout your landscape barefoot, your feet will be better served with smoother stones, such as river rock or pond pebbles. With stone, look for a crushed product in the ¼ to ¾" range. Angular or smooth, stones smaller than that can be tracked into the house, while larger materials are uncomfortable and potentially hazardous to walk on. If it complements your landscaping, use light-colored gravel, such as buff limestone. Visually, it is much easier to follow a light pathway at night because it reflects more moonlight.

Stable edging helps keep the pathway gravel from migrating into the surrounding mulch and soil. When integrated with landscape fabric, the edge keeps invasive perennials and trees from sending roots and shoots into the path. Do not use gravel paths near plants and trees that produce messy fruits, seeds, or other debris that will be difficult to remove from the gravel. Organic matter left on gravel paths will eventually rot into compost that will support weed growth.

A base of compactable gravel under the surface material keeps the pathway firm underfoot. For best results, embed the surface gravel material into the paver base with a plate compactor. This prevents the base from showing through if the gravel at the surface is disturbed. An underlayment of landscape fabric helps stabilize the pathway and blocks weeds, but if you don't mind pulling an occasional dandelion and are building on firm soil, it can be omitted.

Tools & Materials ▸

Mason's string	Edging
Hose or rope	Spikes
Marking paint	Professional-grade
Excavation tools	landscape fabric
Garden rake	Compactable gravel
Plate compactor	Dressed gravel
Sod stripper or	Eye and ear
power sod cutter	protection
Wood stakes	Work gloves
Lumber (1 × 2,	Circular saw
2 × 4)	Maul
Straight 2 × 4	

Construction Details

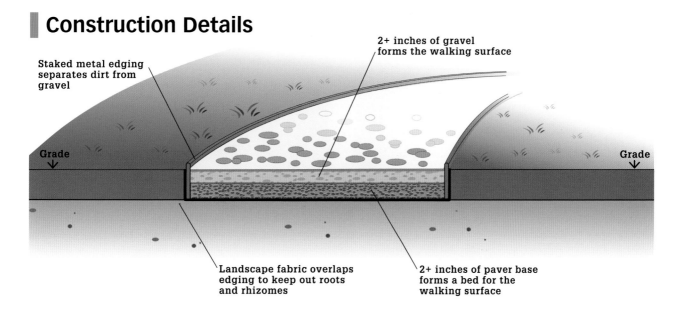

Staked metal edging separates dirt from gravel

2+ inches of gravel forms the walking surface

Grade

Grade

Landscape fabric overlaps edging to keep out roots and rhizomes

2+ inches of paver base forms a bed for the walking surface

To ensure that the edges of the pathway are exactly parallel, create a spacer bar and use it as a guide to install the edging. Start with a piece of 2 × 4 that's a bit longer than the path width. Near one end, cut a notch that will fit snugly over the edging. Trim the spacer so the distance from the notch to the other end is the planned width of the pathway.

How to Create a Gravel Pathway

Lay out one edge of the path excavation. Use a section of hose or rope to create curves, and use stakes and string to indicate straight sections (see pages 140 to 143 for detailed steps on designing and laying out a walkway). Cut 1 × 2 spacers to set the path width and establish the second pathway edge; use another hose and/or more stakes and string to lay out the other edge. Mark both edges with marking paint.

Remove sod in the walkway area using a sod stripper or a power sod cutter (see option, at right). Excavate the soil to a depth of 4 to 6". Measure down from a 2 × 4 placed across the path bed to fine-tune the excavation. Grade the bottom of the excavation flat using a garden rake. *Note: If mulch will be used outside the path, make the excavation shallower by the depth of the mulch.* Compact the soil with a plate compactor.

Option: Use a power sod cutter to strip grass from your pathway site. Available at most rental centers and large home centers, sod cutters excavate to a very even depth. The cut sod can be replanted in other parts of your lawn.

Lay landscaping fabric from edge to edge, lapping over the undisturbed ground on either side of the path. On straight sections, you may be able to run parallel to the path with a single strip; on curved paths, it's easier to lay the fabric perpendicular to the path. Overlap all seams by 6".

Install edging over the fabric. Shim the edging with small stones, if necessary, so the top edge is ½" above grade (if the path passes through grass) or 2" above grade (if it passes through a mulched area). Secure the edging with spikes. To install the second edge, use a 2 × 4 spacer gauge that's been notched to fit over your edging (see page 168).

Stone or vertical-brick edges may be set in deeper trenches at the sides of the path. Place these on top of the fabric also. You do not have to use additional edging with paver edging, but metal (or other) edging will keep the pavers from wandering.

(continued)

Trim excess fabric, then backfill behind the edging with dirt and tamp it down carefully with the end of a 2 × 4. This secures the edging and helps it to maintain its shape.

Add a 2- to 4"-thick layer of compactable gravel over the entire pathway. Rake the gravel flat. Then, spread a thin layer of your surface material over the base gravel.

Tamp the base and surface gravel together using a plate compactor. Be careful not to disturb or damage the edging with the compactor.

Fill in the pathway with the remaining surface gravel. Drag a 2 × 4 across the tops of the edging using a sawing motion, to level the gravel flush with the edging.

Set the edging brick flush with the gravel using a mallet and 2 × 4.

Tamp the surface again using the plate compactor or a hand tamper. Compact the gravel so it is slightly below the top of the edging. This will help keep the gravel from migrating out of the path.

Rinse off the pathway with a hose to wash off dirt and dust and bring out the true colors of the materials.

Stepping stones blend beautifully into many types of landscaping, including rock gardens, ponds, flower or vegetable gardens, or manicured grass lawns.

Pebbled Stepping Stone Path

A stepping stone path is both a practical and appealing way to traverse a landscape. With large stones as foot landings, you are free to use pretty much any type of fill material in between. You could even place stepping stones on individual footings over ponds and streams, making water the temporary infill that surrounds the stones. The infill does not need to follow a narrow path bed, either. Steppers can be used to cross a broad expanse of gravel, such as a Zen gravel panel or a smaller graveled opening in an alpine rock garden.

Stepping stones in a path serve two purposes: they lead the eye, and they carry the traveler. In both cases, the goal is rarely fast, direct transport, but more of a relaxing stroll that's comfortable, slow-paced, and above all, natural. Arrange the stepping stones in your walking path according to the gaits and strides of the people that are most likely to use the pathway. Keep in mind that our gaits tend to be longer on a utility path than in a rock garden.

Sometimes steppers are placed more for visual effect, with the knowledge that they will break the pacing rule with artful clusters of stones. Clustering is also an effective way to slow or congregate walkers near a fork in the path or at a good vantage point for a striking feature of the garden.

In the project featured here, landscape edging is used to contain the loose infill material (small aggregate), however a stepping stone path can also be effective without edging. For example, setting a series of steppers directly into your lawn and letting the lawn grass grow between them is a great choice as well.

Tools & Materials ▸

Mason's string	Thick steppers or
Hose or rope	broad river rocks
Marking paint	with one flat face
Sod stripper	¼ to ½" pond
Excavation tools	pebbles
Hand tamp	2½"-dia. river rock
Wood stakes	Eye and ear
1 × 2 lumber	protection
Straight 2 × 4	Work gloves
Edging	Level
Landscape fabric	Rake
Coarse sand	

Choosing Steppers ▸

Select beefy stones (minimum 2½ to 3½" thick) with at least one flat side. Thinner stepping stones tend to sink into the pebble infill. Stones that are described as stepping stones usually have two flat faces. For the desired visual effect on this project, we chose steppers and 12 to 24" wide fieldstones with one broad, flat face (the rounded face is buried in the ground, naturally).

Fieldstone with a flat face

Steppers

How to Make a Pebbled Stepping Stone Path

Excavate and prepare a bed for the path as you would for the gravel pathway (see pages 169 to 171), but use coarse building sand instead of compactable gravel for the base layer. Screed the sand flat so it's 2" below the top of the edging. Do not tamp the sand. *Tip: Low-profile plastic landscape edging is a good choice because it does not compete with the pathway.*

Moisten the sand bed, then position the stepping stones in the sand, spacing them for comfortable walking and the desired appearance. As you work, place a 2 × 4 across three adjacent stones to make sure they are even with one another. Add or remove sand beneath the steppers, as needed, to stabilize and level the stones.

Pour in a layer of larger infill stones (2"-dia. river rock is seen here). Smooth the stones with a garden rake. The infill should be below the tops of the stepping stones. Reserve about ⅓ of the larger diameter rocks.

Add the smaller infill stones, that will migrate down and fill in around the larger infill rocks. To help settle the rocks, you can tamp lightly with a hand tamper, but don't get too aggressive—the larger rocks might fracture easily.

Scatter the remaining large infill stones across the infill area so they float on top of the other stones. Eventually, they will sink down lower in the pathway and you will need to lift and replace them selectively to maintain the original appearance.

Variations

Move from a formal space to a less orderly area of your landscape by creating a pathway that begins with closely spaced steppers on the formal end and gradually transforms into a mostly-gravel path on the casual end, with only occasional clusters of steppers.

Combine concrete stepping pavers with crushed rock or other small stones for a path with a cleaner, more contemporary look. Follow the same basic techniques used on pages 173 to 174, setting the pavers first, then filling in-between with the desired infill material(s).

Here we use gravel (small aggregate river rock), a common surface for paths and rock gardens, for the tread surfaces. Other tread surfaces include bricks, cobbles, and stepping stones. Even large flagstones can be fit to the tread openings.

Timber Garden Steps

Tools & Materials ▸

Supplies for Timber & Gravel Steps:

Marking paint	Framing square
Mason's string	Drill and ⅜" bit with long shaft
Level	Sledgehammer
Excavation tools	Wood stakes
Hand tamp	Compactable gravel
Circular saw	2 × 4 lumber
Speed square	Landscape timbers
	⅜" landscape spikes
	Gravel

Timberframed steps provide a delightfully simple and structurally satisfying way to manage slopes. They are usually designed with shallow steps that have long runs and large tread areas, that can be filled with a variety of materials. Two popular methods are shown here—gravel and with poured concrete. Other tread surfaces you might consider are bricks, cobbles, and stepping stones. Even large flagstones can be cut to fit the tread openings.

Timber steps needn't follow the straight and narrow, either. You can vary the lengths of the left and right returns to create swooping helical steps that suggest spiral staircases. Or, increase the length of both returns to create a broad landing on which to set pots or accommodate a natural flattening of the slope. Want to soften the steps? Use soil as a base near the sides of the steps and plant herbs or ground cover. Or for a spring surprise, plant daffodils under a light pea gravel top dressing at the edges of the steps.

Timber steps don't require a frost footing, because the wooden joints flex with the earth rather than crack like solid concrete steps would. However, it's a good idea to include some underground anchoring to keep loose muddy soil from pushing the steps forward. To provide longterm stability, the gravel-filled steps shown here are secured to a timber cleat at the base of the slope, while the concrete-filled steps are anchored at the base with long sections of pipe driven into the ground.

Designing steps is an important part of the process. Determine the total rise and run of the hill and translate this into a step size that conforms to this formula: $2 \times (\text{rise}) + \text{run} = 26"$. Your step rise will equal your timber width, that can range from approximately 3½" (for 4 × 4 timbers or 4 × 6 on the flat) to 7¼" or 7½" (for 8 × 8 timbers). See page 143 for more help with designing and laying out landscape steps. As with any steps, be sure to keep the step size consistent so people don't trip.

How to Build Timber & Gravel Garden Steps

Install and level the timber cleat: mark the outline of the steps onto the ground using marking paint. Dig a trench for the cleat at the base of the steps. Add 2 to 4" of compactable gravel in the trench and compact it with a hand tamp. Cut the cleat to length and set it into the trench. Add or remove gravel beneath the cleat so it is level and its top is even with the surrounding ground or path surface.

Create trenches filled with tamped gravel for the returns (the timbers running back into the hill, perpendicular to the cleat and risers). The returns should be long enough to anchor the riser and returns of the step above. Dig trenches back into the hill for the returns and compact 2 to 4" of gravel into the trenches so each return will sit level on the cleat and gravel.

Construction Details: Timber Step Frames

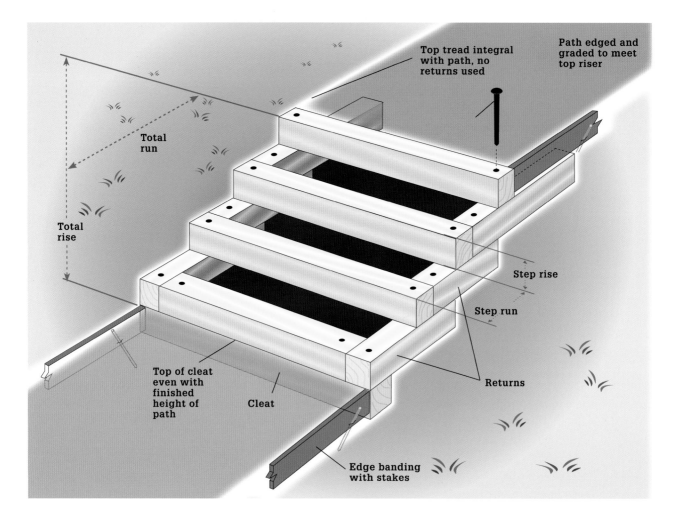

Top tread integral with path, no returns used

Path edged and graded to meet top riser

Total run

Total rise

Step rise

Step run

Top of cleat even with finished height of path

Cleat

Returns

Edge banding with stakes

Cutting Timbers ▶

Large landscape timbers (6 × 6" and bigger) can be cut accurately and squarely with a circular saw, even though the saw's cutting capacity isn't big enough to do the job completely. First, draw cutting lines on all four sides of the timber using a speed square as guide. Next, cut along the line on all four sides with the saw set for maximum blade depth. Finally, use a hand saw to finish the cut. For most DIYers, this will yield a straighter cut than saws that can make the cut in one pass, such as a reciprocating saw.

Cut and position the returns and the first riser. Using a 2 × 4 as a level extender, check to see if the backs of the returns are level with each other and adjust by adding or removing gravel in the trenches. Drill four ⅜"-dia. holes and fasten the first riser and the two returns to the cleat with spikes.

Excavate and add tamped gravel for the second set of returns. Cut and position the second riser across the ends of the first returns, leaving the correct unit run between the riser faces. Note that only the first riser doesn't span the full width of the steps. Cut and position the returns, check for level, then pre-drill and spike the second riser and returns to the returns below.

Build the remaining steps in the same fashion. As you work, it may be necessary to alter the slope with additional excavating or backfilling (few natural hills follow a uniform slope). Add or remove soil as needed along the sides of the steps so that the returns are exposed roughly equally on both sides. Also, each tread should always be higher than the neighboring ground.

Install the final riser. Typically, the last timber does not have returns because its tread surface is integral with the path or surrounding ground. The top of this timber should be slightly higher than the ground. As an alternative, you can use returns to contain pathway material at the top of the steps.

(continued)

Lay and tamp a base of compactable gravel in each step tread area. Use a 2 × 4 as a tamper. For proper compaction, tamp the gravel in 2" or thinner layers before adding more. Leave about 2" of space in each tread for the surface material.

Fill up the tread areas with gravel or other appropriate material. Irregular crushed gravel offers maximum surface stability, while smooth stones, like the river rock seen here, blend into the environment more naturally and feel better underfoot than crushed gravel and stone.

Create or improve pathways at the top and bottom of the steps. For a nice effect, build a loose-fill walkway using the same type of gravel that you used for the steps. Install a railing, if desired or if required by the local building code.

How to Build Timber & Concrete Garden Steps

Mark the sides of the step site with stakes and string. The stakes should be positioned at the front edge of the bottom step and the back edge of the top step.

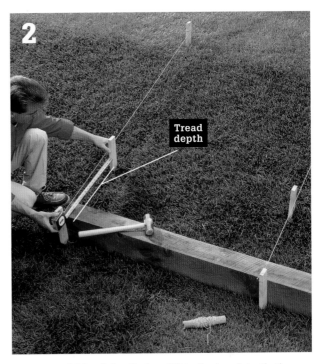

Add the width of the timber (5") to the tread depth, then measure back this distance for the stakes and drive additional stakes to mark the back edge of the first step. Connect these stakes with string to mark the digging area for the first step.

Tools & Materials ›

Supplies for Timber & Concrete Steps:
Mason's string
Excavation tools
Saw
Level
Drill and 1" space bit with bit extension
Maul
Rake
Wheelbarrow
Hoe
Wood float
Concrete edging tool
Stiff brush

Wood stakes
5 × 6 landscape timbers
1" pipe
12" galvanized spikes
Plastic sheeting
Compactable gravel
2 × 4 lumber
Premixed concrete
Seed gravel (½")
Burlap

Excavate for the first step, creating a flat bed with a very slight forward slope, no more than ⅛" from back to front. The front of the excavation should be no more than 2" deep. Tamp the soil firmly.

(continued)

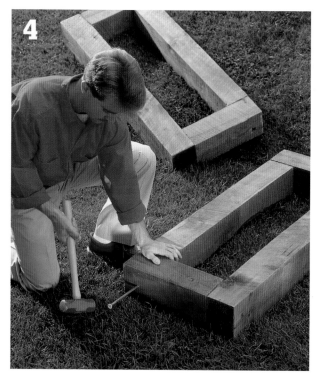

Arrange the timbers to form the step frame and endnail them together with 12" spikes.

Set the timber frame in position. Use a carpenter's square to make sure the frame is square, and adjust as necessary. Drill two 1" guide holes in the front timber and the back timber, 1 ft. from the ends, using a spade bit and bit extension.

Anchor the steps to the ground by driving a 2½-ft. length of ¾" pipe through each guide hole until the pipe is flush with the timber. When pipes are driven, make sure the frame is level from side to side and has the proper forward pitch. Excavate for the next step, making sure the bottom of the excavation is even with the top edge of the installed timbers.

Drive pipes here

Build another step frame and position it in the excavation so the front timber is directly over the rear timber on the first frame. Nail the steps together with three 12" spikes, then drill guide holes and drive two pipes through only the back timber to anchor the second frame.

Continue digging and installing the remaining frames until the steps reach full height. The back of the last step should be at ground level.

Staple plastic over the timbers to protect them from wet concrete. Cut away the plastic so it does not overhang into the frame opening.

Pour a 2"-layer of compactable gravel subbase into each frame, and use a 2 × 4 to smooth it out.

Mix concrete in a wheelbarrow, adding just enough water so the concrete holds its shape when sliced with a trowel.

Shovel concrete into the bottom frame, flush with the top of the timbers. Work the concrete lightly with a garden rake to help remove air bubbles, but do not overwork the concrete.

(continued)

13

Screed the concrete by dragging a 2 × 4 across the top of the frame. If necessary, add concrete to low areas and screed again until the surface is smooth and free of low spots.

14

While the concrete is still wet, scatter mixed gravel on the surface. Sand-and-gravel suppliers and garden centers sell colorful gravel designed for seeding. For best results, select a mixture with stones no larger than ½" in diameter.

15

Press the seeded gravel into the surface of the concrete using a concrete float, until the tops of the stone are flush with the surface of the concrete. Remove any concrete that spills over the edges of the frame using a trowel.

16

Pour concrete into the remaining steps, screeding and seeding each step before moving on to the next. For a neater appearance, use an edging tool (inset) to smooth the cracks between the timbers and the concrete as each step is finished.

When the sheen disappears from the poured concrete (4 to 6 hours after pouring), use a float to smooth out any high or low spots in each step. Be careful not to force seeded gravel too far into the concrete. Let the concrete dry overnight.

After concrete has dried overnight, apply a fine mist of water to the surface, then scrub it with a stiff brush to expose the seeded gravel.

Variation: To create a nonslip surface on smooth concrete without seeding, draw a stiff-bristled brush or broom once across the concrete while it is still wet.

Remove the plastic from the timbers, and cover the concrete with burlap. Allow the concrete to cure for several days, spraying it occasionally with water to ensure even curing. *Note: Concrete residue can be cleaned from timbers using a solution of 5% muriatic acid and water.*

Stone steps blend natural elegance and beauty for a stunning landscape feature in any yard. Depending on how stylized the design is and the type of stone (natural shaped or cut square), the steps can enhance either a formal or casual outdoor living area.

Flagstone Garden Steps

Flagstone steps are perfect structures for managing natural slopes. Our design consists of broad flagstone treads and blocky ashlar risers, commonly sold as wall stone. The risers are prepared with compactable gravel beds on which the flagstone treads rest. For the project featured here, we purchased both the flagstone and the wall stone in their natural split state (as opposed to sawn). It may seem like overkill, but you should plan on purchasing 40 percent more flagstone, by square foot coverage, than your plans say you need. The process of fitting the stones together involves a lot of cutting and waste.

The average height of your risers is defined by the height of the wall stone available to you. These rough stones are separated and sold in a range of thicknesses (such as 3 to 4"), but hand-picking the stones helps bring them into a tighter range. The more uniform the thicknesses of your blocks, the less shimming and adjusting you'll have to do. (Remember, all of the steps must be the same size, to prevent a tripping hazard.) You will also need to stock up on slivers of rocks to use as shims to bring your risers and returns to a consistent height; breaking and cutting your stone generally produces plenty of these.

Flagstone steps work best when you create the broadest possible treads: think of them as a series of terraced patios. The goal, once you have the stock in hand, is to create a tread surface with as few stones as possible. This generally means you'll be doing quite a bit of cutting to get the irregular shapes to fit together. For a more formal look, cut the flagstones along straight lines so they fit together with small, regular gaps.

Tools & Materials ▸

Tape measure	Wall stone
Mason's string	Flagstone
Marking paint	Stone chisels
Line level	Stone and block
Torpedo level	adhesive
4-ft. level	Rubber mallet
Excavation tools	Eye and ear
Maul	protection
Hand tamp	Work gloves
Wood stakes	Small brush
Lumber (2 × 4,	Banker box (see
4× 4)	page 82)
Straight 2 × 4	Spade
Landscape fabric	Granite or polymeric
Compactable gravel	sand
Coarse sand	

Construction Details

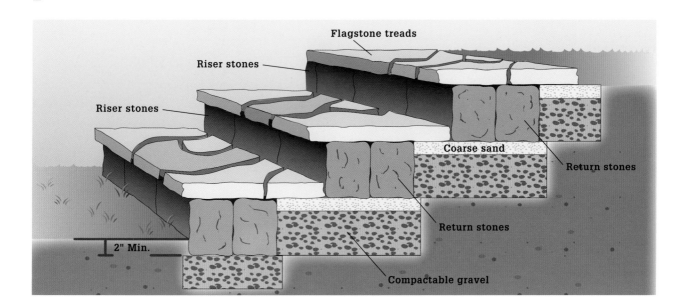

Pave the slope. Sometimes the best solution for garden steps is simply to lay some broad, flat rocks down on a pathway more or less as you find it. Make some effort to ensure that the surface of each rock is relatively flat and safe to walk on. Do not use this approach on steep slopes (greater than 2 in 12) or in heavily traveled areas.

These terraces are made from large flagstone steppers supported by stacked riser stones. They function as steps in managing the slope, but they look and feel more like a split-level patio. For a natural look and the best visual effect, terrace-type steps should mimic the topography of your yard.

Cut-limestone blocks that are roughly uniform in size are laid in a step formation to create a stately passageway up this small hill. A hand-formed mortar cap adorns the sides of the outdoor stairway for a more finished appearance.

Stacked slabs cannot be beat for pure simplicity, longevity, and ease of maintenance. The initial cost is high, and stacking stones that weigh several hundred pounds (or more) does require professionals with heavy equipment. But once these lovely garden steps are in place they'll stay put for generations with hardly any attention beyond a simple hosing off.

How to Build Flagstone Garden Steps

Measure the height and length of the slope to calculate the rise and run dimensions for each step (see page 143 for help with designing and laying out steps). Plot the footprint of your steps on the ground using marking paint. Purchase wall stones for your risers and returns in a height equal to the rise of your steps. Also buy flagstone (with approx. 40% overage) for the step treads.

Begin the excavation: for the area under the first riser and return stones, dig a trench to accommodate a 4"-layer of gravel, plus the thickness of an average flagstone tread. For the area under the back edge of the first step's tread and the riser and return stones of the second step, dig to accommodate a 4"-layer of gravel, plus a 1"-layer of sand. Compact the soil with a 2 × 4 or 4 × 4.

Add a layer of compactable gravel to within 1" of the planned height and tamp. Add a top layer of compactable gravel and level it side to side and back to front. This top layer should be a flagstone's thickness below grade. This will keep the rise of the first step the same as the following steps. Leave the second layer of gravel uncompacted for easy adjustment of the riser and return stones.

Set the riser stones and one or two return stones onto the gravel base. Level the riser stones side to side by adding or removing gravel as needed. Level the risers front to back with a torpedo level. Allow for a slight up-slope for the returns (the steps should slope slightly downward from back to front so the treads will drain). Seat the stones firmly in the gravel with a hand maul, protecting the stone with a wood block.

(continued)

Line the excavated area for the first tread with landscape fabric, draping it to cover the insides of the risers and returns. Add layers of compactable gravel and tamp down to within 1" of the tops of the risers and returns. Fill the remainder of the bed with sand and level it side to side with a 2 × 4. Slope it slightly from back to front. This layer of sand should be a little above the first risers and returns so that the tread stones will compact down to sit on the wall stones.

Set the second group of risers and returns: first, measure the step/run distance back from the face of your first risers and set up a level mason's string across the sand bed. Position the second-step risers and returns as you did for the first step, except these don't need to be dug in on the bottom because the bottom tread will reduce the risers' effective height.

Fold the fabric over the tops of the risers and trim off the excess. Set the flagstone treads of the first step like a puzzle, leaving a consistent distance between stones. Use large, heavy stones with relatively straight edges at the front of the step, overhanging the risers by about 2".

Fill in with smaller stones near the back. Cut and dress stones where necessary using stone chisels and a maul or mason's hammer (see pages 82 to 83 for tips on cutting stone). Finding a good arrangement takes some trial and error. Strive for fairly regular gaps, and avoid using small stones as they are easily displaced. Ideally, all stones should be at least as large as a dinner plate.

Adjust the stones so the treads form a flat surface. Use a level as a guide, and add wet sand under thinner stones or remove sand from beneath thicker stones until all the flags come close to touching the level and are stable.

Shim between treads and risers with thin shards of stone. (Do not use sand to shim here). Glue the shards in place with block and stone adhesive. Check each step to make sure there is no path for sand to wash out from beneath the treads. You can settle smaller stones in sand with a mallet, but cushion your blows with a piece of wood.

Complete the second step in the same manner as the first. The bottoms of the risers should be at the same height as the bottoms of the tread on the step below. Continue building steps to the top of the slope. *Note: The top step often will not require returns.*

Fill the joints between stones with sand by sweeping the sand across the treads. Use coarse, dark sand such as granite sand, or choose polymeric sand, which resists washout better than regular builder's sand. Inspect the steps regularly for the first few weeks and make adjustments to the heights of stones as needed.

Boardwalk

Whether as a garden path or a high-traffic walkway, a boardwalk can add a touch of elegance to any yard. The simplicity of this project's design makes it an easy solution to many walkway problems. Frames measuring 29 × 45" are constructed from pressure-treated lumber and recessed in trenches along the project area. Cedar decking boards conceal the frame, creating a lovely walkway surface through your yard.

The boardwalk should be built on a relatively flat stretch of ground. For greater stability, fasten the frames together with ⁵⁄₁₆ × 2½" galvanized lag screws driven through both sides of the end boards.

Tools & Materials ▸

Mason's string
Excavation tools
Hand tamp
Circular saw
Drill
Ratchet wrench
T-bevel
Wood stakes
Professional-grade landscape fabric
Compactable gravel

2 × 4 pressure-treated lumber
Galvanized deck screws (2½, 3")
⁵⁄₁₆ × 2½" galvanized lag screws with washers
¾ × 6 cedar decking boards
¼" plywood spacer

A boardwalk is great for creating a level, elevated path over uneven ground or low-lying areas that tend to get washed out or swampy during wet weather. To increase the height of a boardwalk, use wide lumber (2 × 6, 2 × 8, or larger) for the frame construction.

How to Build a Boardwalk

Lay out the edges of the walk using stakes and string. Dig a trench 4½" deep × 34" wide, running the full length of the site. Cover the trench base with landscape fabric, overlapping strips by at least 6". Add a 2"-layer of compactable gravel, rake it flat and smooth, and compact it evenly with a hand tamp.

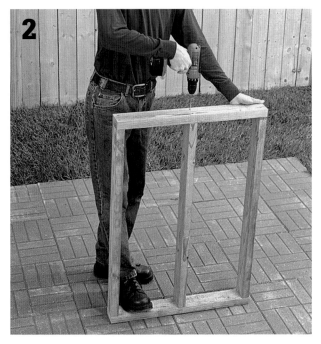

Construct each boardwalk frame with three 2 × 4 stringer pieces cut at 42" and two end pieces cut at 29". Assemble the frame as shown here, using pairs of 3" deck screws driven through the end boards and into the stringers (drill pilot holes for the screws). For shorter frames at the end of a run, cut the stringers 3" shorter than the total length needed.

Install the frames. Lay the frames into the trench, butting them end to end with their side edges aligned. Fasten the frames together with pairs of lag screws driven through pilot holes on both sides of the mating end boards. Backfill along the side edges of the frames with gravel for drainage.

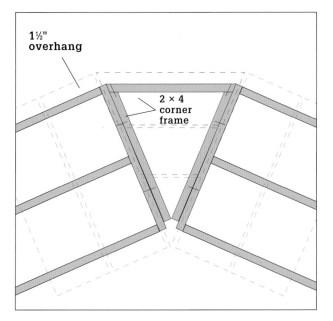

1½"
overhang

2 × 4
corner
frame

Variation: To create a corner, position two frame sections at the angle in the trench with the front corners touching. Tack a string between the back corners, then measure and cut pressure-treated 2 × 4s to size for one corner stringer and two nailers. Use a T-bevel to find the angles created by the turn, and miter-cut the ends of each board to the angle of the turn. Fasten the pieces together with 3" deck screws. For the decking, use the same angle to miter-cut across the face of the boards. Cut them to size as you go.

Deck the frame. Cut the decking boards at 32". Starting at one end of the walk, position each board so it overhangs the frames by 1½" on both sides. Drill pilot holes and fasten the board to the frame with pairs of 2½" deck screws driven into each stringer. Install the remaining deck boards using a plywood spacer to gap the boards ¼" apart.

Patio Rooms & Amenities

Featuring several projects for turning an ordinary open patio into a custom outdoor room, this chapter is all about making the most of your patio space. A patio room is more of a design concept than a specific type of structure. The idea is to enhance a space with just the right elements to make it more usable, comfortable, or private.

If your patio feels just a little too exposed or if the layout could use some definition and a sense of enclosure, an overhead or side screening could be just what's needed to complete your outdoor oasis. If you like the protection of a covered patio but don't want a solid roof overhead, then a patio enclosure may be the perfect alternative. Or, for a truly classic patio overhead, you can't beat the look and subtle shading of a cedar arbor. You'll even find a project for transforming the undesirable space under a second-story deck into a pleasant covered patio.

As for amenities, we've included two of the most popular back yard projects: an outdoor kitchen for the patio and landscape lighting, that can be used on a patio or walkway. If you're building a new patio and want to include either of these amenities, be sure to plan for the utility hookups early in the process, in case you need to run lines under the patio surface.

In this chapter:

- Under-Deck Patio
- Patio Enclosure
- Patio Arbor & Trellis
- Screened Patio Room
- Outdoor Kitchen
- Low-voltage Patio & Landscape Lighting

Under-Deck Patio

Second-story walk-out decks can be a mixed blessing. On top, you have an open, sun-filled perch with a commanding view of the landscape. The space below the deck, however, is all too often a dark and chilly nook unprotected from water runoff. As a result, an under-deck area often ends up as wasted space or becomes a holding area for seasonal storage items or the less desirable outdoor furniture.

But there's an easy way to reclaim all that convenient outdoor space—by installing a weatherizing ceiling system that captures runoff water from the deck above, leaving the area below dry enough to convert into a versatile outdoor room. You can even enclose the space to create a screened-in patio room.

The under-deck system featured in this project is designed for do-it-yourself installation. Its components are made to fit almost any standard deck and come in three sizes to accommodate different deck-joist spacing (for 12", 16", and 24" on-center spacing). Once the system is in place, the under-deck area is effectively "dried in", and you can begin adding amenities like overhead lighting, ceiling fans, and speakers to complete the outdoor room environment.

The system works by capturing water that falls through the decking above and channeling it to the outside edge of the deck. Depending on your plans, you can let the water fall from the ceiling panels along the deck's edge, or you can install a standard rain gutter and downspout to direct the water to a single exit point on the ground (see pages 203 to 205).

Tools & Materials ▸

4-ft. level	1" stainless
Chalk line	steel screws
Drill	Rain gutter system
Aviation snips	(optional)
Hacksaw	Ear and eye
(for optional	protection
rain gutter)	Work gloves
Under-deck	Tape measure
ceiling system	Carpenter's pencil
Waterproof	Color-matched
acrylic caulk	caulk
(and caulk gun)	

Made of weather-resistant vinyl, this under-deck system creates an attractive, maintenance-free ceiling—the perfect shelter for an open-air or enclosed patio space below.

Design Tips

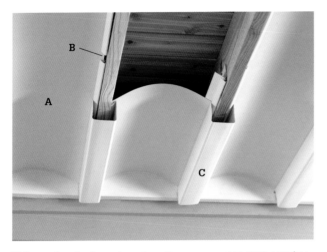

This under-deck system (see Resources, page 250) consists of four main parts: the joist rails mount to the deck joists and help secure the other components. The collector panels (A) span the joist cavity to capture water falling through the deck above. Water flows to the sides of the panels where it falls through gaps in the joist rails (B) and into the joist gutters (C) (for interior joists) and boundary gutters (for outer joists). The gutters carry the water to the outside edge of the deck.

For a finished look, paint the decking lumber that will be exposed after the system is installed. Typically, the lower portion of the ledger board (attached to the house) and the outer rim joist (at the outer edge of the deck) remain exposed.

Consider surrounding architectural elements when you select a system for sealing off the area below your deck. Here, the under-deck system is integrated with the deck and deck stairs both visually and functionally.

How to Install an Under-deck System

Check the undersides of several deck joists to make sure the structure is level. This is important for establishing the proper slope for effective water flow.

If your deck is not level, you must compensate for this when setting the ceiling slope. To determine the amount of correction that's needed, hold one end of the level against a joist and tilt the level until it reads perfectly level. Measure the distance from the joist to the free end of the level. Then, divide this measurement by the length of the level. For example, if the distance is ¼" and the level is 4 ft. long, the deck is out of level by ¹⁄₁₆" per foot.

To establish the slope for the ceiling system, mark the ends of the joists closest to the house. Measure up from the bottom 1" for every 10 ft. of joist length (or approximately ⅛" per ft.) and make a mark. Add or subtract the out-of-level factor from step 2.

Create each slope reference line using a chalk line. Hold one end of the chalk line at the mark made in Step 3, and hold the other end at the bottom edge of the joist where it meets the rim joist at the outside edge of the deck. Snap a reference line on all of the joists.

Install vinyl flashing along the ledger board in the joist cavities. Attach the flashing with 1" stainless steel screws. Caulk along the top edges of the flashing where it meets the ledger and both joists using quality, waterproof acrylic caulk. Also caulk the underside of the flashing for an extra layer of protection.

Begin installing the joist rails, starting 1" away from the ledger. Position each rail with its bottom edge on the chalk line, and fasten it to the joist at both ends with 1" stainless steel screws; then add one or two screws in between. Avoid over-driving the screws and deforming the rail. Leaving a little room for movement is best.

Install the remaining rails on each joist face, leaving a 1½" (minimum) to 2" (maximum) gap between rails. Install rails along both sides of each interior joist and along the insides of each outside joist. Trim the final rail in each row as needed using aviation snips.

Measure the full length of each joist cavity, and cut a collector panel ¼" shorter than the cavity. This allows room for expansion of the panels. For narrower joist cavities, trim the panel to width following the manufacturer's sizing recommendations.

(continued)

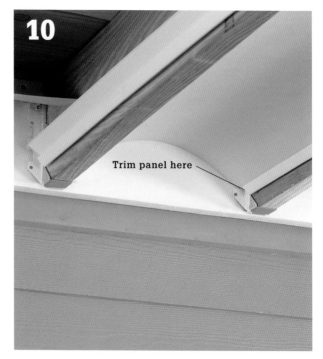

Scribe and trim the collector panels for a tight fit against the ledger board. Hold a carpenter's pencil flat against the ledger, and move the pencil along the board to transfer its contours to the panel. Trim the panel along the scribed line.

Trim the corners of the collector panels as needed to accommodate joist hangers and other hardware. This may be necessary only at the house side of the joist cavity; at the outer end, the ¼" expansion gap should clear any hardware.

Trim panel here

Install the collector panels, starting at the house. With the textured side of the panel facing down, insert one side edge into the joist rails, and then push up gently on the opposite side until it fits into the opposing rails. When fully installed, the panels should be tight against the ledger and have a ¼" gap at the rim joist.

Prepare each joist gutter by cutting it ¼" shorter than the joist it will attach to (if the joists rest on a structural beam, see page 202). On the house end of each gutter, trim the corners of the flanges at 45°. This helps the gutter fit tightly to the ledger.

13

Cut four or five ⅛" tabs into the bottom surface at the outside ends of the gutters. This helps promote the drainage of water over the edge of the gutter.

14

Caulk here

Attach self-adhesive foam weatherstrip (available from the manufacturer) at the home-end of each joist gutter. Run a bead of caulk along the foam strip to water-seal it to the gutter. The weather strip serves as a water dam.

15

Install each joist gutter by spreading its sides open slightly while pushing the gutter up onto the joist rails until it snaps into place. The gutter should fit snugly against the collector panels. The gutter's home-end should be tight against the ledger with the ¼" expansion gap at the rim joist.

16

Prepare the boundary gutters following the same steps used for the joist gutters. Install each boundary gutter by slipping its long, outside flange behind the joist rails and pushing up until the gutter snaps into place. Install the boundary gutters working from the house side to the outer edge of the deck.

(continued)

17

Run a bead of color-matched caulk along the joint where the collector panels meet the ledger board. This is for decorative purposes only and is not required to prevent water intrusion.

18

If collector panels are misshapen because the joist spacing is too tight, free the panel within the problem area, then trim about ⅛" from the side edge of the panel. Reset the panel in the rails. If necessary, trim the panel edge again in slight increments until the panel fits properly.

Working Around Beams ▸

Decking

Rim joist

Collector panel

Joist gutter

Deck beam

Post

Rain gutter

For decks that have joists resting on top of a structural beam, stop the joist gutters and boundary gutters 1½" short of the beam. Install a standard rain gutter along the house-side of the beam to catch the water as it exits the system gutters. (On the opposite side of the beam, begin new runs of joist gutters that are tight against the beam and stop ¼" short of the rim joist. The joist rails and collector panels should clear the beam and can be installed as usual.) Or, you can simply leave the overhang area alone if you do not need water runoff protection below it.

Runoff Gutters

A basic gutter system for a square or rectangular deck includes a straight run of gutter channel with a downspout at one end. Prefabricated vinyl or aluminum gutter parts are ideal for this application. Gutter channels are commonly available in 10-ft. and 20-ft. lengths, so you might be able to use a single channel without seams. Otherwise, you can join sections of channel with special connectors. Shop around for the best type of hanger for your situation. If there's limited backing to support the back side of the channel or to fasten into, you may have to use strap-type hangers that can be secured to framing above the gutter.

Runoff gutters are installed at the ends of the under-deck channels to capture runoff water and redirect it away from the enclosed area through downspouts.

How to Install an Under-deck Runoff Gutter

1

Snap a chalk line onto the beam or other supporting surface to establish the slope of the main gutter run. The line will correspond to the top edge of the gutter channel. The ideal slope is $\frac{1}{16}$" per foot. For example, with a 16-ft.-long gutter, the beginning is 1" higher than the end. The downspout should be located just inside the low end of the gutter channel. Mark the beam at both ends to create the desired slope, then snap a chalk line between the marks. The high end of the gutter should be just below the boundary gutter in the ceiling system.

(continued)

2

Install a downspout outlet near the end of the gutter run so the top of the gutter is flush with the slope line. If you plan to enclose the area under the deck, choose an inconspicuous location for the downspout, away from traffic areas.

3

Install hanger clips (depending on the type of hangers or support clips you use, it is often best to install them before installing the gutter channel). Attach a hanger every 24" so the top of the gutter will hang flush with the slope line.

Tip ▶

Gutters come in several material types, including PVC, enameled steel and copper. In most cases you should try to match the surrounding trim materials, but using a more decorative material for contrast can be effective.

4

Cut sections of gutter channel to size using a hacksaw. Attach an end cap to the beginning of the main run, then fit the channel into the downspout outlet (allowing for expansion, if necessary) and secure the gutter in place.

5

Join sections of channel together, if necessary, for long runs using connectors. Install a short section of channel with an end cap on the opposite side of the downspout outlet. Paint the area where the downspout will be installed if it is unpainted.

6

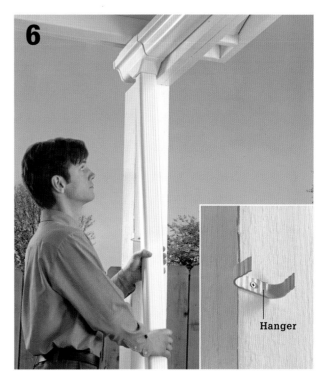

Hanger

Cut the downspout piping to length and fasten an elbow fitting to its bottom end. Attach the downspout to the downspout outlet, then secure the downspout to a post or other vertical support using hangers (inset).

7

Cut a drainpipe to run from the downspout elbow to a convenient drainage point. Position the pipe so it directs water away from the house and any traffic areas. Attach the pipe to the downspout elbow. Add a splash block, if desired.

Routing Drainpipes ▸

You may have to get a little creative when routing the downspout drain in an enclosed porch or patio. Shown here, two elbows allow for a 90° turn of the drainpipe.

Patio Enclosure

If you like the openness and plentiful light of a patio but want more protection from rain and strong winds, this stylish, contemporary patio shelter may be just what you're looking for. Designed as a cross between an open-air arbor or pergola and an enclosed three-season porch, this patio structure has clear glazing panels on its roof and sides, allowing plenty of sunlight through while buffering the elements and even blocking harmful UV rays.

The roof of the patio shelter is framed with closely spaced 2 × 4 rafters to create the same light-filtering effects of a slatted arbor roof. The rafters are supported by a doubled-up 2 × 10 beam and 4 × 6 timber posts. Because the shelter is attached to the house, the posts are set on top of concrete foundation piers, or footings, that extend below the frost line. This prevents any shifting of the structure in areas where the ground freezes in winter.

The patio shelter's side panels cut down on wind while providing a degree of privacy screening. Their simple construction means you can easily alter the dimensions or locations of the panels to suit your own plans. In the project shown, each side has two glazing panels with a 3½" space in between, for airflow. If desired, you can use a single sheet of glazing across the entire side section. The glazing is held in place with wood strips and screws so they can be removed for seasonal cleaning.

Slats of white oak sandwich clear polycarbonate panels to create walls that block the wind without blocking light and views.

Building against a solid wall and not in front of a patio door makes the space inside this contemporary shelter much more usable. The corrugated roof panels (see Resources, page 250) made of clear polycarbonate allow light to enter while keeping the elements out.

Patio Enclosure Plans

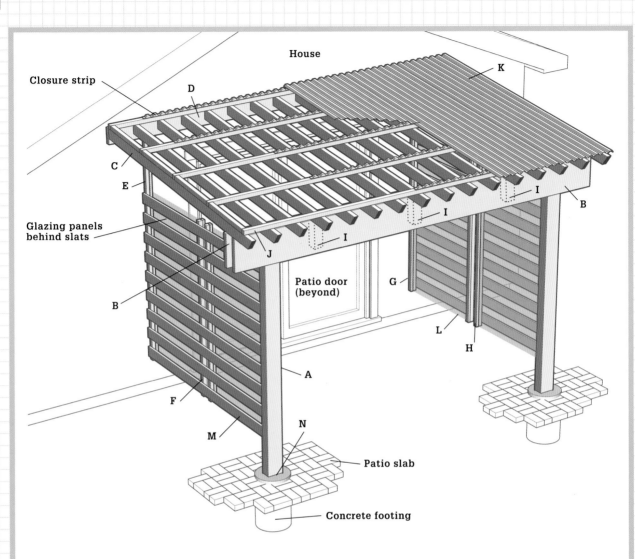

House

Closure strip

K

D

C

E

Glazing panels
behind slats

B

J

I

I

I

I

B

Patio door
(beyond)

G

L

H

A

F

M

N

Patio slab

Concrete footing

Plan your own patio shelter based on the requirements set by the local building code. Your city's building department or a qualified building professional can help you with the critical structural specifications, such as the size and depth of the concrete post footings, the sizing of beam members, and the overall roof construction. The building department will help make sure your shelter is suitable for the local weather conditions (particularly wind and snow loads).

Cutting List

Key	Part	No.	Size	Material	Key	Part	No.	Size	Material
A	Post	2	3½ × 5½ × 144"	4 × 6 treated pine	H	Slat cleat cap	4	¾ × 1½ × 60"	1 × 2 pine
B	Beam member	2	1½ × 9¼ × 120"*	2 × 10 treated pine	I	Beam blocks	3	3½ × 3½ × 8"	4 × 4 pine
C	Rafter	16	1½ × 3½ × 120"*	2 × 4 pine	J	Purlin	14	1½ × 1½ × 120"	2 × 2 pine
D	Ledger	1	1½ × 5½ × 144"	2 × 6 treated pine	K	Roof panel	6	¼ × 26 × 96"	Corrugated polycarbonate
E	Back post	2	1½ × 1½ × 96"*	2 × 2 pine	L	Side panel	4	¼ × 36 × 58"	Clear polycarbonate
F	Slat cleat	4	1½ × 1½ × 60"	2 × 2 pine	M	Slat	18	¾ × 3½ × 80"*	White oak
G	Back post cap	2	¾ × 1½ × 96"*	1 × 2 pine	N	Post base	2	1½ × 3½ × 3½"	

*Size listed is prior to final trimming

Tools & Materials

Chalk line
4-ft. level
Plumb bob
Mason's string
Digging tools
Concrete mixing tools
Circular saw
Ratchet wrench
Line level
Reciprocating saw or handsaw
Drill with bits
Finish application tools
Gravel
12"-dia. concrete tube forms
Concrete mix
⅝"-dia. J-bolts
⅜ × 4" corrosion resistant lag screws
Flashing
Silicone caulk
Corrosion-resistant metal post bases and hardware

Lumber
Corrosion-resistant 16d and 8d common nails
½"-dia. corrosion-resistant lag bolts and washers
Exterior wood glue or construction adhesive
Corrosion-resistant framing anchors (for rafters)
Deck screws (1½, 3")
Polycarbonate roofing panels
Clear polycarbonate panels
Closure strips
Roofing screws with EPDM washers
Roofing adhesive/sealant
Wood finishing materials
Neoprene weatherstripping
Scrap lumber
Exterior wood stain
Stakes
Eye and ear protection
Hammer
Caulk gun
Table saw, router, or circular saw
Work gloves

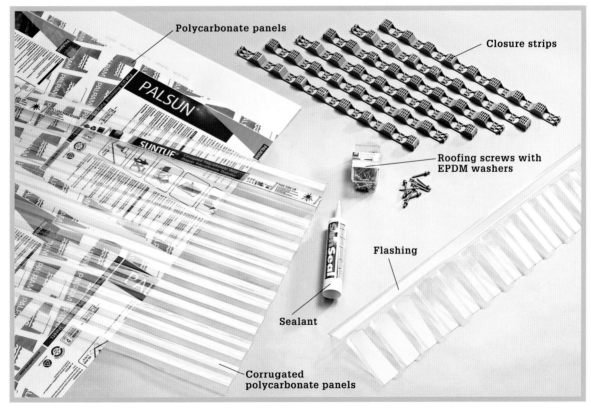

The roofing and side glazing panels of the patio shelter are made with tough polycarbonate materials. The corrugated roofing panels allow up to 90% light transmission while blocking virtually 100 percent of harmful UV rays. The flat side panels offer the transparency of glass but are lighter and much stronger than glass. Also shown is: wall flashing designed to be tucked under siding; closure strips that fit between the 2 × 2 purlins and the corrugated roof panels; self-sealing screws and polycarbonate caulk.

How to Build a Patio Enclosure

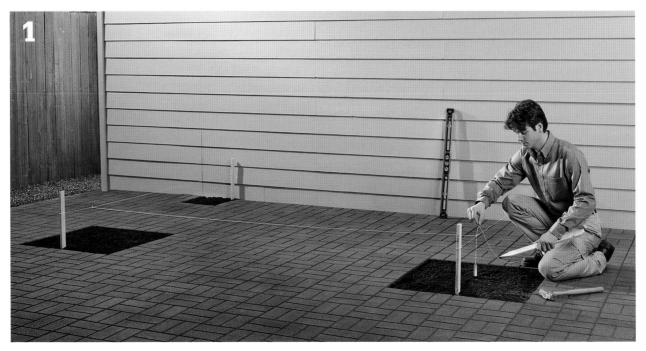

Mark the layout for the ledger board on the house wall. Lay out the post footing locations in the patio area. To mark the cutout for the ledger board, include the width of the ledger board, plus the height of the roofing, plus 1½" for the flashing. The length of the cutout should be 1" longer than the length of the ledger board (12 ft. as shown). Plumb down from the ends of the ledger, then measure in to mark the locations of the post centers. At each of these points, run a perpendicular string line from the house out to about 2 ft. beyond the post locations. Set up a third string line, perpendicular to the first two, to mark the centers of the posts. Plumb down from the string line intersections and mark the post centers on the ground with stakes.

Dig a hole for a concrete tube form at each post location following the local building code for the footing depth. Add 6" of gravel and tamp it down. Position the tube forms so they are plumb and extend at least 2" above the ground. Backfill around them with soil and compact thoroughly.

Fill the tube forms with concrete and screed it level with the tops of the forms. At each post-center location, embed a J-bolt into the wet concrete so it extends the recommended distance above the top of the form. Let the concrete cure.

4

Cut out the house siding for the ledger board using a circular saw. Cut only through the siding, leaving the wall sheathing. *Note: If the sheathing is fiberboard instead of plywood, you may have to remove the fiberboard; consult your local building department.* Replace any damaged building paper covering the sheathing.

5

Stain the wood parts before you begin installing the shelter closure strips and panels. We used a black, semitransparent deck and siding stain.

6

Apply a protective finish to the wood slats as desired. We used a semitransparent deck stain.

(continued)

Install the ledger. First, slip corrugated roof flashing or metal roof flashing behind the siding above the ledger cutout so the vertical flange extends at least 3" above the bottom of the siding. Cut the ledger board to length. Fasten the ledger to the wall using ⅜ × 4" lag screws driven through counterbored pilot holes at each wall-stud location. Seal over the screw heads and counterbores with silicone caulk.

Anchor the post bases to the concrete footing, securing them with the base manufacturer's recommended hardware. Make sure the bases are aligned with each other and are perpendicular to the house wall.

Cut off the bottom ends of the posts so they are perfectly square. Set each post in its base and hold it plumb. Fasten the post to the base using the manufacturer's recommended fasteners. Brace the posts with temporary bracing. *Note: You will cut the posts to length in a later step.*

10

Cut a pattern rafter from 2 × 4 lumber using the desired roof slope to find the angle cut for the top end. Angle the bottom end as desired for decorative effect. Set the rafter in position so its top end is even with the top of the ledger and its bottom end passes along the side of a post. Mark along the bottom edge of the rafter onto the post. Repeat to mark the other post. Use a string and line level to make sure the post marks are level with each other.

11

Cut the inner beam member to length from 2 × 10 lumber, then bevel the top edge to follow the roof slope. Position the board so its top edge is on the post markings, and it overhangs the posts equally at both ends (12" of overhang is shown). Tack the board in place with 16d nails.

12

Cut the outer beam member to length from 2 × 10 lumber. Bevel the top edge following the roof slope, and remove enough material so that the bottom edges of the two beam members will be level with each other. Tack the member in place with nails.

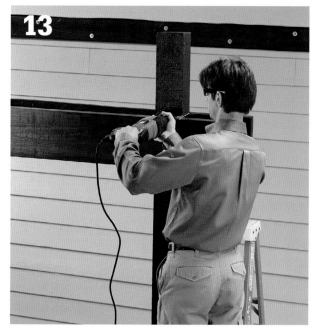

13

Anchor the beam members together and to the posts with pairs of ½"-dia. lag bolts and washers. Cut the posts off flush with the tops of the beam members using a handsaw or reciprocating saw.

(continued)

14

Trim the cutoff post pieces to length and use them as blocking between the beam members. Position the blocks evenly spaced between the posts and fasten them to both beam members with glue and 16d nails. *Note: Diagonal bracing between the posts and beam may be recommended or required in some areas; consult your local building department.*

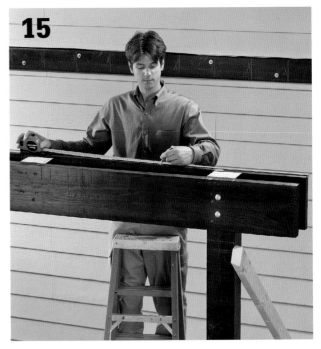

15

Mark the rafter layout onto the ledger and beam. As shown here, the rafters are spaced 9½" apart on center. The two outer rafters should be flush with the ends of the ledger and beam.

16

Install metal framing anchors onto the ledger for securing the top rafter ends using the anchor manufacturer's recommended fasteners. Use the pattern rafter or a block to position the anchors so the rafters will be flush with the top of the ledger.

17

Use the pattern rafter to mark the remaining rafters and then cut them. Install the rafters one at a time. Fasten the top ends to the metal anchor using the recommended fasteners. Fasten the bottom ends to both beam members by toenailing one 8d nail through each rafter side and into the beam member.

18

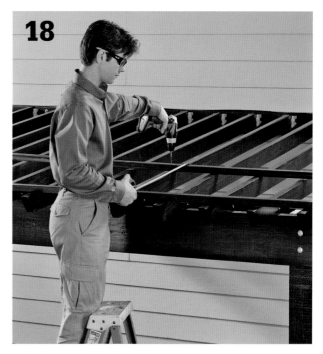

Install the 2 × 2 purlins perpendicular to the rafters using 3" deck screws. Position the first purlin a few inches from the bottom ends of the rafters. Space the remaining purlins 24" on center. The ends of the purlins should be flush with the outside faces of the outer rafters.

19

Add 2 × 2 blocking between the purlins along the outer rafters, and fasten them with 3" deck screws. This blocking will support the vertical closure strips for the roof panels.

20

Starting at one side of the roof, install the roof panel closure strips over the purlins using the manufacturer's recommended fasteners. Begin every run of strips from the same side of the roof, so the ridges in the strips will be aligned.

(continued)

Add vertical closure strips over the 2 × 2 purlin blocking to fill in between the horizontal strips.

Position the first roofing panel along one side edge of the roof. The inside edge of the panel should fall over a rafter. If necessary, trim the panel to length or width following the manufacturer's recommendations.

Drill pilot holes, and fasten the first panel to the closure strips with the recommended type of screw and rubber washer. Fasten the panel at the peak (top) of every other corrugation. Drive the screws down carefully, stopping when the washer contacts the panel but is not compressed. This allows for thermal expansion of the panel.

Apply a bead of the recommended adhesive/sealant (usually supplied by the panel manufacturer) along the last trough of the roofing panel. Set the second panel into place, overlapping the last troughs on both panels. Fasten the second panel. Install the remaining panels using the same procedure. Caulk the seam between the roof panels and the roof flashing.

25

Blade
guard
removed
for clarity

To create channels for the side glazing panels, mill a rabbet into each of the eight vertical 2 × 2 cleats. Consult the glazing manufacturer for the recommended channel size, making sure to provide space for thermal expansion of the panels. Mill the rabbets using a table saw, router, or circular saw. Stop the rabbets so the bottom edges of the panels will be even with, or slightly above, the bottom edge of the lowest side slat.

Tip ▶

If you do not have wall flashing designed to work with the roof profile, place closure strips upside down onto the roof panels and run another bead of adhesive/sealant over the tops of the strips. Work the flashing down and embed it into the sealant. Seal along all exposed edges of the ledger with silicone caulk.

26

Position a cleat on each post at the desired height, with the cleat centered from side to side on the post. The rabbeted corner should face inside the shelter. Fasten the cleats to the posts with 3" deck screws. Fasten two more cleats to the house wall so they are aligned and level with the post cleats.

27

Cut the side slats to length to fit between the posts and the house wall. Mark the slat layouts onto the outside faces of the cleats, and install the slats with 1½" deck screws or exterior trim-head screws. Space the slats 3½" apart or as desired.

(continued)

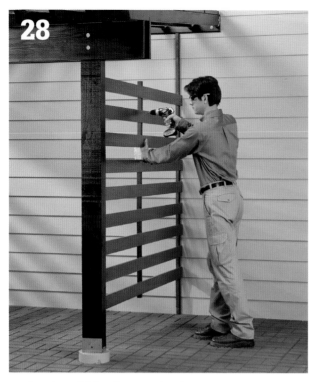

28

Fasten the middle cleats to the slats on each side, leaving about 3½" of space between the cleats (or as desired). The cleats should overhang the top and bottom slats by 1½" (or as desired).

Tip ▶

Used for decorative accent slats on this patio shelter, white oak is a traditional exterior wood that was employed for boatbuilding as well as outdoor furnishings. Although it requires no finishing, we coated the white oak with a dark, penetrating wood stain to bring out the grain.

29

Cut the cap strips for the glazing panels from 1 × 2 material (or rip down strips from the 1 × 4 slat material). Position each cap over a cleat and drill evenly spaced pilot holes through the cap and into the cleat. Make sure the holes go into the solid (non-rabbeted) portion of the cleat. Drill counterbores, too (left). Drive screws to attach the post caps (right).

Trim the side glazing panels to size following the manufacturer's directions. Apply neoprene or EPDM stripping or packing to the side edges of the panels. Fit each panel into its cleat frame, cover the glazing edges with the 1 × 2 caps, and secure the caps with 1½" deck screws. *Note: If the glazing comes with a protective film, remove the film during this step as appropriate and make sure the panel is oriented for full UV protection.*

Option: Add a 2 × 4 decorative cap on the outside face of each post. Center the cap side-to-side on the post and fasten it with 16d casing nails.

Patio Arbor & Trellis

A traditional framed arbor can have a transformative effect on a patio. Architecturally, an arbor frames the patio space, providing a sense of shelter and a room-like feel without closing it off from the outdoors. The overhead framework of an arbor can be used to support climbing plants for additional shading in the summer months.

In the following projects, you'll see how to build a classic four-post arbor and then how to add an additional post and supplemental lattice panels to one side of the structure. A patio arbor like this is easiest to build if it's freestanding or not attached directly to your house. Permanent structures attached to a house are subject to stricter building code requirements than freestanding projects. The arbor shown here is built upon new concrete footings located just outside the edges of the patio. Because the arbor is freestanding, the footings did not need to extend below the frost line (as they would for an attached structure).

Tools & Materials ▸

Tape measure	Ladder	Posthole digger	Clamps
Mason's string	Shovel	Handsaw	4 × 8-ft. lattice panels
Line level	Mortar box	Cedar framing lumber	Galvanized brads
Torpedo level	Concrete	(2 × 4, 4 × 4, 2 × 8,	Fence brackets
Carpenter's square	Post anchors	2 × 6, 2 × 2)	4d galvanized nails
Speed square	½"-dia. carriage bolts	Straightedge	2 × 2 lattice molding
Drill with ½" bit and	Rafter ties	Eye and ear protection	Pencil
bit extension	J-bolts with nuts	16d galvanized nails	Chalk line
Circular saw	and washers	⅜ × 4" lag screws	Hammer
Ratchet-socket set	Work gloves	2½" deck screws	Fence brackets

Arbor structures make a dramatic visual statement when constructed over an ordinary patio. They also help cut down on wind and sun and create a more pleasant outdoor environment.

A Simple Arbor for a Garden Patio ▸

A freestanding arbor can go almost anywhere in a landscape, making it a great addition to a remote garden patio. You can design and locate the arbor to shelter only a portion of a patio, or it can cover the entire area. The arbor design described here is simpler than the one on the following pages and is typical of freestanding arbors in a garden or landscape.

The arbor shown here is relatively small. You can easily adapt the design to different sizes, but don't space the posts more than 8 ft. apart. If you want to build a larger arbor, add additional posts between the corner posts. Before you begin construction, check your local building code for footing depth requirements and setback restrictions.

The basics of building a freestanding arbor are as follows. First, lay out the location of the posts using stakes and string. Make sure the layout is square by measuring from corner to corner and adjusting the layout until these diagonal measurements are equal. Dig postholes at the corners to the required depth using a posthole digger and fill each hole with 6" of gravel.

Next, position the posts in the holes. To brace them in a plumb position, tack support boards to the posts on adjoining faces. Adjust the posts as necessary until they're plumb. Drive a stake into the ground, flush against the base of each 2 × 4. Drive deck screws through the stakes, into the 2 × 4s.

Mix one bag of dry concrete to anchor each post. Immediately check to make sure the posts are plumb, and adjust as necessary until the concrete begins to harden. Let the concrete cure for at least 24 hours.

Measure, mark, and cut all the lumber for the arbor. Cut a 3 × 3" notch off the bottom corner of each tie beam, a 2 × 2" notch off the bottom corner of each 2 × 4 rafter, and a 1 × 1" notch off the bottom corner of each cross strip. Position a tie beam against the outside edge of a pair of posts, 7 ft. above the ground. Position the beam to extend about 1 ft. past the post on each side. Level the beam, then clamp it into place with wood screw clamps. Drill pilot holes and attach the tie beam to the posts with 3" lag screws.

Use a line level to mark the opposite pair of posts at the same height as the installed tie beam. Attach the remaining tie beam. Cut off the posts so they're level with the tops of the tie beams.

Next, attach the rafters to the tops of the tie beams using rafter ties and galvanized nails. Beginning 6" from the ends of the tie beams, space the rafters 2 ft. apart, with the ends extending past each tie beam by 1 ft. Position a cross strip across the top of the rafters, beginning 6" from the ends of the rafters. Center the strip so it extends past the outside rafters by about 6". Drill pilot holes through the cross strip and into the rafters. Attach the cross strip with galvanized screws. Add the remaining cross strips, spacing them 1 ft. apart. Finish your arbor by applying wood sealer or protectant.

This version of a freestanding post-and-slat arbor is a 5 × 5-ft. cedar structure with an extended overhead.

How to Build a Patio Arbor

Create footings for the arbor posts by digging a hole at least twice the size of the post bottom and at least 12" deep. Fill with concrete, and set a J-bolt in each concrete footing. We positioned the J-bolts so the edges of the posts are flush with the patio.

Allow the footings to harden for at least one day, then attach the post anchor hardware to the J-bolts. Cut and install the arbor posts—for most arbors, 4 × 4 posts are large enough. Cut posts longer than the planned height, and brace them with 2 × 4 braces so they are plumb. Leave the braces in place until the beams and rafters are secured in position.

Use a square to mark the cutting lines for the posts at the desired height. Mark the height of the arbor onto the posts at one end, then use a line level to transfer the height mark onto the posts at the other end. With a square, mark cutting lines on all four sides of each post. Trim the posts at the cutting lines using a handsaw. Have a helper steady the post from below while you cut. *Note: You may use a power saw, like a cordless circular saw, to cut off the post tops, but only if your ladder provides enough elevation that you can work from above the cutting line.*

Cut beam members from 2 × 8 stock. Because we used two beam members each at the front and back of the project, we cut four beam members. To create a 6" overhang at each side, cut the beam members 12" longer than the distance between the outside edges of the posts. Mark all beam members with a carpenter's square, then gang-cut them with a circular saw and a straightedge.

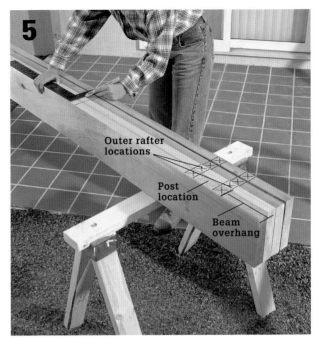

Turn beams on edge, and mark locations for the rafters. Rafters should be no more than 24" apart. Start by marking the outermost rafters—our plan called for a rafter at the inside and outside edge of each post. Don't forget to include the beam overhang in the layout.

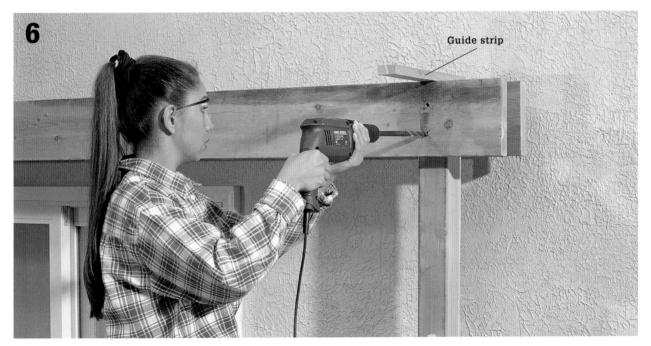

Fasten the beam members to the posts at the front and back of the arbor. Screw a guide strip securely to the top of each post, then position the beam members and hold them in place temporarily by driving a screw down through the guide strip and into the top of each beam member. When installing beam pairs, as shown here, use a pair of carriage bolts with washers and nuts at each beam/post joint. Attach a ½" bit with a bit extension to your drill, and drill holes for the carriage bolts through both the beam members and the post.

(continued)

7

Pound ½"-dia. carriage bolts through the holes. Carriage bolts should be ½ to 1" longer than the combined widths of the outer rafters and the beam. For this project, we used a 7"-long bolt. Slip a washer and nut onto the end of the carriage bolt and tighten with a ratchet. Remove the guide strip.

8

Measure and mark 2 × 6 rafters to fit on top of the beams, perpendicular to the house. For best appearance, rafters should overhang the beams by at least 6". Cut with a circular saw. For added visual appeal, mark an angled cut of about 30° at the end of one rafter, then cut off with a circular saw. Use the rafter as a template to transfer the angle to the other rafters.

9

Rafter tie

Install the rafters on top of the beams at the rafter layout marks. Position the rafters so the angled ends are at the front of the project, with the shorter side resting on the beam. Use metal rafter ties, mounted to the beams, and deck screws to attach the rafters. *Option: Because the metal rafter ties can be quite visible in the finished product, you may prefer to toenail the rafters in place with 16d galvanized nails.*

10

Beam mark

18"

18"

Crossbrace location

Post mark

Mark the posts and beams for crossbraces. From the inside corner of each post/beam joint, mark an equal distance (about 18") on the beam and the post. For crossbraces that fit between rafters, measure from the post mark to the top of the rafter, following the line created between the post mark and the beam mark. For crossbraces that fit flush with the post and the beam, measure from the post mark to the beam mark for the inside dimension of the crossbrace.

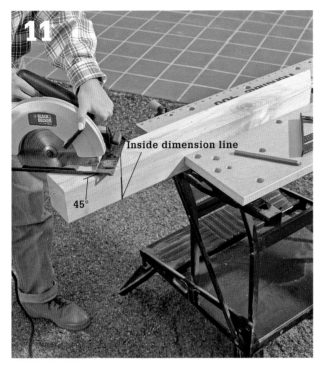

Mark the inside dimensions for the crossbraces onto a piece of lumber of the same type as the posts (here, 4 × 4). Use a square to draw 45° cutting lines away from each end point of the inside dimension. Cut along these lines with a circular saw to make the crossbraces.

Install the crossbraces. Tack the crossbraces in position, then attach them with ⅜ × 4" lag screws. If the crossbrace is fitted between the rafters, drive the lag screws through the counterbored pilot holes in the rafter and into the crossbrace at the top. Attach with lag screws at each joint. Drive lag screws through the counterbored pilot holes that are perpendicular to the post or rafter.

Install the arbor slats on top of the rafters. We used 2 × 2 cedar spaced at 4" intervals. Include an overhang of at least 6". Attach the arbor slats with 2½" deck screws driven down through the slats and into the rafters.

Adding a Trellis to an Arbor

Add a lattice-panel trellis to an arbor structure for a more decorative appearance. Using manufactured lattice panels and lattice molding and hanging the panels with metal fence-panel hangers makes the job inexpensive and quick. Or, you can build your own lattice and frame. Plant climbing garden varieties and train them up the trellis to embellish the design. Lattice panels also increase your patio's privacy, create a windbreak, and add additional shade for sunny areas.

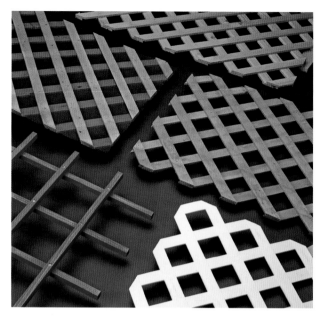

Most building centers carry cedar, pressure-treated, and vinyl lattice in 2 × 8-ft. and 4 × 8-ft. panels. Standard lattice panels are ¾" thick. For a customized look, build your own lattice panels from exterior-rated lumber.

How to Add a Trellis to an Arbor

If the planned trellis is wider than 4 ft., you will need additional support posts. Install posts using the same materials and techniques used for the corner posts of the arbor (see page 222). If possible, install the posts so the lattice panels on either side of each post will be equal in size.

Measure the openings between the posts to determine the sizes for the lattice panels. Generally, panels should be sized so they are installed below the crossbraces between posts. Leave a few inches of open space beneath the panels at ground level. Mark the locations of the panel tops onto the posts using a level to make sure the tops are even.

Subtract 1½" from the frame opening dimensions, and cut the lattice panels to size. To cut lattice panels, sandwich each panel between two boards near the cutting line to prevent the lattice from separating. Clamp the boards and the panel together and cut with a circular saw.

Miter-cut 2 × 2 lattice molding to frame the lattice panels. The finished width of the panel should be ½" narrower than the opening. Nail one vertical and one horizontal frame piece together with galvanized brads. Set the lattice panel into the channels, and attach the other frame pieces. Secure the lattice panels into the molding by driving brads through the molding and into the lattice at 12" intervals.

Attach three fence brackets to the posts, evenly spaced, on each side of the opening using 4d galvanized nails. On the top two brackets, bend the bottom and top flanges flat against the post. Bend all outside flanges flat, away from the post, to allow installation of the lattice panel.

Set the panels in the brackets, and bend the hanger flanges back to their original positions. Drive 1" galvanized nails through the flanges of the fence hangers and into the frames of the lattice panels.

Screened Patio Room

A screening system is an ingeniously simple and effective way to enclose a covered patio—leaving you free to enjoy the outdoors at any time of day without the annoyance of insects and other pests. A basic system includes three main components: a base channel that mounts directly to the patio-roof posts, railings, and other framing members (as applicable); the screening (and spline); and a trim cap that snaps in place over the base channel to cover the screen edges and add a finished look to the installation. The base cap pieces are made to go together, but the screen and spline may need to be purchased separately. Be sure to follow the system manufacturer's specifications for screen type and spline size. Screen systems are typically compatible with standard fiberglass and aluminum screen materials.

With the system shown in this project, each piece of screen is secured into the base channels using standard vinyl or rubber spline and a spline roller. The screen goes up quickly and easily after a little practice, and it doesn't have to be perfectly tight right away; when the cap pieces are snapped on, they add tension to the screening, pulling it tight from all sides of the opening. This does a good job of eliminating the unsightly sag that occurs all too quickly with standard stapled-up screening. Replacing screen sections also is much easier with a screen system: just remove the surrounding cap pieces, pull out the spline, and install a new piece of screen.

Tools & Materials ▸

Pruning sheers or aviation snips	Corrosion-resistant deck screws (1, 3½")	Power hand planer	Work gloves
Drill with bits	Screening	Exterior construction adhesive (and caulk gun)	Carpenter's square
Spline roller	Spline cord	Concrete anchors or deck screws	Tape measure
Utility knife	2 × 4 lumber or composite equivalent	Eye and ear protection	Wood shims
Rubber mallet	Straightedge	Clamps	Hinges and fasteners
Screen system components		Circular saw	Galvanized finish nails
Level			Screen door handles, latches, and closer hardware

Screen systems are quick, easy products for screening in covered patios, including under-deck spaces like the patio shown here.

Cladding Posts ▶

With their textures and grain, plain wood posts are right at home in many parts of many homes. But when you combine them with gleaming new white vinyl-based products, they can look a little rough. One way to make your patio-roof posts blend better when you're installing under-deck or screening systems is to clad them and paint them to match. Traditionally, clear dimensional lumber is used for the cladding. But to get seamless results, this often means you need to cut complicated dado-rabbet joints that run all the way from top to bottom at each corner. Then, you need to sand thoroughly and apply several coats of paint. An easier option for making all of your screen system parts match is to clad posts with one-piece PVC post cladding (see Resources, page 250). The product shown here is designed to fit around a 6 × 6" post. On the interior surface it is kerfed but the exterior vinyl surface is solid. This way, it can be bent around corners crisply and seamlessly.

Vinyl cladding can be wrapped around wood posts seamlessly.

Spline-based screening systems are available at home centers and hardware stores and through many websites. Screen Tight, the system shown here (see Resources, page 250), is made with UV-resistant PVC and is available with trim colors of white, gray, beige, and brown. Parts of the system include: stretchable spline cord (A); spline roller (B); adhesive for bonding rigid vinyl (C); storm door handles (D); storm door hinges (E); 1" corrosion-resistant screws (F); screw-eye door latch (G); deck screws (H); decorative cap screws (I); track cap (J); track base (K); composite 2 × 4 (L); fiberglass screening (M).

How to Install a Screening System

Begin installing the track backers that frame the openings you will be screening. You may use pressure-treated 2 × 4s or 2 × 2s. For a long-lasting and low-maintenance framework, we used composite 2 × 4-sized backers that came with the screen system materials. These products are quite new and are not rated for structural use. Attach the backers to the inside faces of the posts, centered, using exterior construction adhesive and 3½" deck screws.

Secure sole plates to the patio or porch floor using construction adhesive and appropriate fasteners (use concrete anchors for concrete, stone, or paver patios and use deck screws for wood and nonwood decking).

Attach cap plates to the beam or joist at the top of the installation area, leaving 1½" between plates to create recesses for the vertical backers.

Install the vertical track backer members with the top ends fitted in the gaps you left in the cap plate. Make sure the vertical members are plumb and then drive deck screws toenail style through the members and into the sole plate. Also drive screws up at angles through the vertical members and into the beam or joist at the top of the area. Drill pilot holes.

5

Install the door header and the horizontal track backers using adhesive and deck screws. Locate the horizontal members 36 to 42" above the ground.

6

Cut a base channel to length for each vertical member in the screen frame. At the tops of the posts, hold the base channel back to allow room for the horizontal channels, if applicable (see step 12 photo). This results in less cutting of the cap trim later. Cut the channels using pruning shears or aviation snips.

7

Fasten the vertical channel pieces to the framing with 1" corrosion-resistant screws. Drive a screw into each predrilled hole in the channel, then add a screw 2" from each end. Drive each screw in snugly but not so far that it warps the channel.

8

Cut the horizontal base channels to length and install them with screws. The butted joints where the horizontal channels meet the verticals don't have to be precise or tight-fitting.

(continued)

9

Begin installing the screen by positioning a full piece of screening over an opening so it overlaps several inches on all sides. Secure the screen into the horizontal base channel at one of the top corners using spline cord. You can plan to run the spline around the corners or cut it off at the ends as needed.

10

Embed the spline at the starting point, where it should fit fully into the groove of the base channel. Use a spline roller. Then, using one hand to pull the screen taut, press the spline into place to secure the screen along the top of the opening.

11

Secure the screen along both sides, then along the bottom using the same technique as for the top. When you're finished, the screen should be flat and reasonably tight, with no sagging or wrinkling. If you make a mistake or the screen won't cooperate, simply remove the spline and start over.

12

Trim off the excess screening with a sharp utility knife. Fiberglass screen cuts very easily, so control the knife carefully at all times. Repeat steps as needed to screen in the remaining openings.

13

Install the trim caps over the base channels, starting with the vertical pieces. Working from the bottom up, center the cap over the base, then tap it into place using a rubber mallet. *Tip: If you have a continuous horizontal band along the top of the screening, install those trim pieces before capping the verticals.*

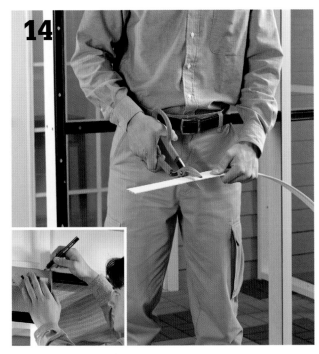

Cut the cap pieces to length as you install them. Mark cutting lines with a pencil, and make the cuts with pruning shears or aviation snips. If desired, use a square to mark a straight cutting line across the face or backside of the trim cap (inset).

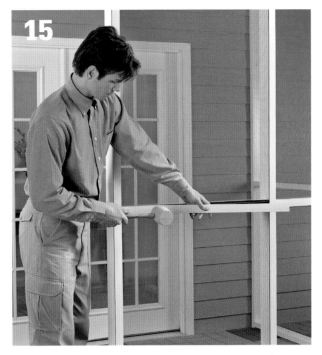

Install the horizontal pieces once the vertical cap pieces are in place using the same techniques. Butt the horizontals tight against the verticals to start each piece, and then trim it to length as you approach the opposite end.

Complete the screening project by installing a screen door. A low-maintenance vinyl door provides a good match with the finish of the vinyl trim cap, but a traditional painted wood door is also appropriate. See pages 234 to 235 for door installation steps.

Option: To protect the screening from being damaged by pets, kids, or other causes, make lattice frames and install them in the framed areas.

How to Install a Screen Door

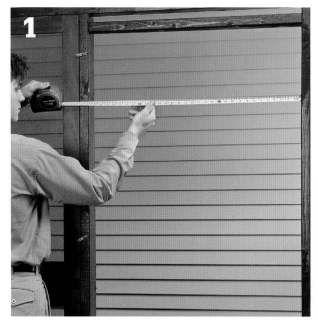

Measure the door opening. The new screen door should be ¼ to ⅜" narrower and ¼ to ½" shorter than the opening. Plan to trim the door, if necessary, for proper clearance. Some vinyl doors should not be cut, while others may be cut only a limited amount. If the door is vinyl, check with the manufacturer.

To trim the height of a door, mark the cutting line, then clamp a straightedge to the door to guide your circular saw for a straight cut. For wood doors, score deeply along the cutting line with a utility knife before setting up the straightedge; this prevents splintering on the top side when cutting across the grain.

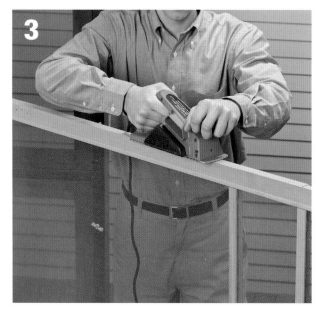

To trim the width of a wood door, it's usually best to remove material from the hinge side, which is less visible. Mark a full-length cutting line, and make the cut with a circular saw. Or, you can use a power hand planer to trim off material from the edge (shown in photo). Use sand paper or a file to round-over the cut side (and bottom, if applicable) edges to match the uncut edges and to prevent splinters.

Test-fit the door in the opening using wood shims along the bottom to raise the door to the right height. Center the door from side to side; the reveal here should be about ⅛" on each side.

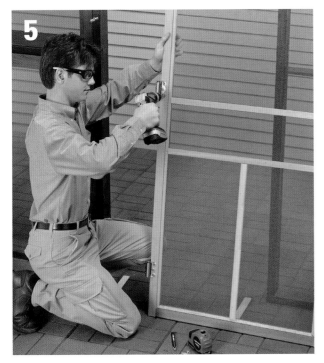

Install surface-mount hinges to the door using screws driven into pilot holes (three hinges is preferable, but two will work for most doors). Position the top hinge about 7" from the top of the door, the bottom hinge about 10" from the bottom, and the middle hinge halfway between the other two.

Hang the door. Set the door into the opening using shims at the sides to establish equal reveals. Mark and drill pilot holes for the hinges, then screw the hinges to the side jamb or post to hang the door.

Install doorstop molding around the sides and top of the door opening using galvanized finish nails if your screen door is not prehung. Position the stops so the outer door face is flush with the outer jamb edges, trim, or door posts, as applicable. Install the stop along the top of the opening first, then along the sides.

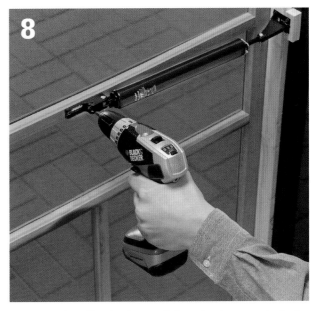

Add door handles, latches, and closer hardware as desired, following the manufacturer's instructions. A closer is a good idea to prevent the door from being left open and admitting insects. Closers come in a range of types, including spring-loaded hinges, hydraulic pistons, and old-fashioned extension springs. Most also have a stop chain that prevents the door from blowing all the way open.

Patio Kitchen

With its perfect blend of indoor convenience and alfresco atmosphere, it's easy to see why the outdoor kitchen is one of today's most popular patio projects. In terms of design, outdoor kitchens can take almost any form, but most are planned around the essential elements of a built-in grill and convenient countertop surfaces (preferably on both sides of the grill). Secure storage inside the cooking cabinet is another convenience many outdoor cooks find indispensable.

The kitchen design in this project combines all three of these elements in a moderately sized cooking station that can fit a variety of patio configurations. The structure is freestanding and self-supporting, so it can be installed almost anywhere you can provide a stable foundation. In this project, the kitchen is built on top of an existing concrete patio slab. If you don't have a suitable slab, you can pour a new concrete patio (see pages 89 to 99). Once your kitchen is built, adding a table and chairs or a casual sitting area might be all you need to complete your dining accommodations.

Made almost entirely of inexpensive masonry materials, this kitchen is perfectly suited to the outdoors. Masonry is noncombustible, is not damaged by water, and can easily withstand decades of outdoor exposure. In fact, a little weathering makes masonry look even better. The kitchen's structural cabinet is built with concrete block, while the countertop is made of poured concrete and is cast in place over two layers of cementboard (for a total profile thickness of 3"). The block sides of the cabinet provide plenty of support for the countertop, as well as a good surface for applying the stucco finish. You could also finish the cabinet with veneer stone or tile.

This practical outdoor kitchen has just what the serious griller needs—a built-in grill and plenty of countertop space for preparing and serving meals. At just over 8 ft. long and about 3 ft. wide, the kitchen can fit almost anywhere on a standard concrete patio.

Tools & Materials ▸

Chalk line	Deck screws
Pointed trowel	(2½ and 3")
Mortar mixing tools	Stucco lath
Level	Silicone caulk (caulk
Mason's string	gun)
Circular saw with	Release agent
masonry blade	Countertop concrete
Mason's chisel	mix
Hand maul	Base coat stucco
Utility knife	Finish coat stucco
Straightedge	Jigsaw with
Square-notched	remodeler's blade
trowel	(optional)
Metal snips	Eye and ear
Wood float	protection
Steel finishing	Concrete colorant
trowel	(optional)
Drill with masonry	Hammer
bit	Abrasive brick,
Concrete blocks	diamond pad, or
Mortar mix	sandpaper
Metal	Food-safe concrete
reinforcement	sealer
Steel angle lintels	Work gloves
½" cementboard	Cabinet doors and
Lumber (2 × 4 and	hardware
2 × 6)	Hawk

Construction Details

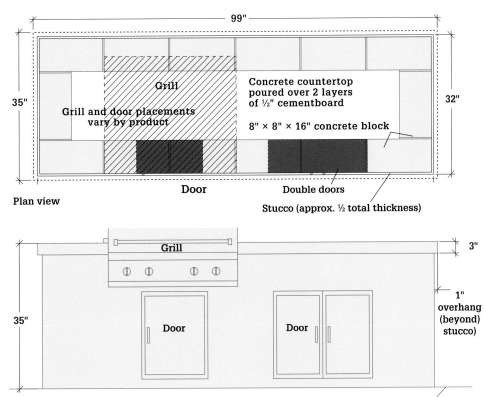

99"

35"

Grill

Grill and door placements vary by product

Concrete countertop poured over 2 layers of ½" cementboard

8" × 8" × 16" concrete block

32"

Door

Double doors

Stucco (approx. ½ total thickness)

Plan view

Grill

Door

Door

35"

3"

1" overhang (beyond) stucco)

Front elevation

Concrete slab (reinforced as required)

The basic structure of this kitchen consists of five courses of standard 8" × 8" × 16" concrete block. Two mortared layers of ½" cementboard serve as a base for the countertop. The 2"-thick poured concrete layer of the countertop extends 1½" beyond the rough block walls and covers the cementboard edges. The walls receive a two-coat stucco finish, which can be tinted during the mixing or painted after it cures. Doors in the front of the cabinet provide access to storage space inside and to any utility connections for the grill. The kitchen's dimensions can easily be adjusted to accommodate a specific location, cooking equipment, or doors and additional amenities.

Planning a Kitchen Project ▶

Whether you model your project after the one shown here or create your own design, there are a few critical factors to address as part of your initial planning:

Foundation: Check with your local building department about foundation requirements for your kitchen. Depending on the kitchen's size and location, you may be allowed to build on top of a standard 4"-thick reinforced concrete patio slab, or you might need a foundation with frost footings or a "floating" or slab-on-grade foundation.

Grill & door units: You'll need the exact dimensions of the grill, doors, and any other built-in features before you draw up your plans and start building. When shopping for equipment, keep in mind its utility requirements and the type of support system needed for the grill and other large units. Some grills are drop-in and are supported only by the countertop; others must be supported below with a non-combustible, load-bearing material such as concrete block or a poured concrete platform.

Utility hookups: Grills fueled by natural gas require a plumbed gas line, and those with electric starters need an outdoor electrical circuit, both running into the kitchen cabinet. To include a kitchen sink, you'll need a dedicated water line and a drain connection (to the house system, directly to the city sewer, or possibly to a dry well on your property). Outdoor utilities are strictly governed by building codes, so check with the building department for requirements. Generally, the rough-in work for utilities is best left to professionals.

Kitchen grills may be supplied by a natural gas line connected to the house supply or by a refillable propane tank stored inside the kitchen's cabinet area.

How to Build a Patio Kitchen

Prepare the patio slab or foundation by cleaning the surface thoroughly to remove all dirt, oil, paint, or sealer that could prevent a good bond with the mortar. Snap chalk lines representing the outer edges of the block walls.

Dry-lay the first course of block along the chalk lines to test the layout. If desired, use 2"- or 4"-thick solid blocks under the door openings. Adjust the layout lines as needed, and mark the exact locations of the door openings.

Set the first course of block into a mortar bed, compressing the mortar to ⅜". Lay the second course of block, following a running bond (1 over 2) pattern. Cut blocks as needed for the openings by scoring the cutting lines with a circular saw and masonry blade and splitting the block with a mason's chisel.

Continue laying up the wall, adding reinforcing wire or rebar if required by local building codes. Instead of tooling the mortar joints for a concave profile, use a trowel to slice excess mortar from the blocks. This creates a flat surface that's easier to cover with stucco.

Install steel angle lintels to span over the door openings. If an opening is in line with a course of block, mortar the lintels in place on top of the block. Otherwise, use a circular saw with a masonry blade to cut channels for the horizontal leg of the angle. Lintels should span 6" beyond each side of an opening. Slip the lintel into the channels, and then fill the block cells containing the lintel with mortar to secure the lintel in place. Lay a bed of mortar on top of the lintels, then set block into the mortar. Complete the final course of block in the cabinet and let the mortar cure.

Cut two 8-ft.-long sheets of cementboard to match the outer dimensions of the block cabinet. Apply mortar to the tops of the cabinet blocks and then set one layer of cementboard into the mortar. If you will be installing a built-in grill or other accessories, make cutouts in the cementboard with a utility knife or a jigsaw with a remodeler's blade.

Cut pieces to fit for a second layer of cementboard. Apply a bed of mortar to the top of the first panel, and then lay the second layer pieces on top, pressing them into the mortar so the surfaces are level. Let the mortar cure.

(continued)

To create a 1½" overhang for the countertop, build a perimeter band of 2 × 4 lumber; this will serve as the base of the concrete form. Cut the pieces to fit tightly around the cabinet along the top. Fasten the pieces together at their ends with 3" screws so their top edges are flush with the bottom of the cementboard.

Cut vertical 2 × 4 supports to fit snugly between the foundation and the bottom of the 2 × 4 band. Install a support at the ends of each wall and evenly spaced in between. Secure each support with angled screws driven into the band boards.

Build the sides of the countertop form with 2 × 6s cut to fit around the 2 × 4 band. Position the 2 × 6s so their top edges are 2" above the cementboard, and fasten them to the band with 2½" screws.

Form the opening for the grill using 2 × 6 side pieces (no overhang inside opening). Support the edges of the cementboard along the grill cutout with cleats attached to the 2 × 6s. Add vertical supports as needed under the cutout to keep the form from shifting under the weight of the concrete.

12

13

Cut a sheet of stucco lath to fit into the countertop form, leaving a 2" space along the inside perimeter of the form. Remove the lath and set it aside. Seal the form joints with a fine bead of silicone caulk and smooth with a finger. After the caulk dries, coat the form boards (not the cementboard) with vegetable oil or another release agent.

Dampen the cementboard with a mist of water. Mix a batch of countertop concrete mix, adding colorant to the mix if desired. Working quickly, fill along the edges of the form with concrete, carefully packing it down into the overhang portion by hand.

14

15

Fill the rest of the form halfway up with an even layer of concrete. Lay the stucco lath on top, then press it lightly into the concrete with a float. Add the remaining concrete so it's flush with the tops of the 2 × 6s.

Tap along the outsides of the form with a hammer to remove air bubbles trapped against the inside edges. Screed the top of the concrete with a straight 2 × 4 riding along the form sides. Add concrete as needed to fill in low spots so the surface is perfectly flat.

(continued)

16

After the bleed water disappears, float the concrete with a wood or magnesium float. The floated surface should be flat and smooth but will still have a somewhat rough texture. Be careful not to overfloat and draw water to the surface.

17

A few hours after floating, finish the countertop as desired. A few passes with a steel finishing trowel yields the smoothest surface. Hold the leading edge of the trowel up and work in circular strokes. Let the concrete set for a while between passes.

18

Moist-cure the countertop with a fine water mist for three to five days. Remove the form boards. If desired, smooth the countertop edges with an abrasive brick and/or a diamond pad or sandpaper. After the concrete cures, apply a food-safe sealer to help prevent staining.

19

Prepare for door installation in the cabinet. Outdoor cabinet doors are usually made of stainless steel, and are typically installed by hanging hinges or flanges with masonry anchors. Drill holes for masonry anchors in the concrete block, following the door manufacturer's instructions.

20

Finish installing and hanging the doors. Test the door operations and make sure to caulk around the edges with high-quality silicone caulk. *Note: Doors shown here are best installed before the stucco finish is applied to the cabinet. Other doors may be easier to install following a different sequence.*

21

Begin finishing the cabinet walls by dampening the concrete block and applying a ⅜"-thick base coat of stucco, following the manufacturer's directions. Apply an even layer over the wall, and then smooth the surface with a wood float. Moist-cure the stucco for 48 hours or as directed by the manufacturer.

22

Apply a finish coat of tinted stucco that's at least ⅛" thick. Evenly saturate the base coat stucco surface with water prior to applying the finish coat. Texture the surface as desired. Moist-cure the stucco for several days as directed.

23

Set the grill into place, make the gas connection, then check it carefully for leaks. Permanently install the grill following the manufacturer's directions. The joints around grills are highly susceptible to water intrusion; seal them thoroughly with an approved caulk to help keep moisture out of the cabinet space below.

Low-voltage Patio Lighting

Thanks to the many inexpensive and easy-to-install lighting kits and fixtures available, outdoor lighting has become a standard feature in today's home landscapes. A good lighting plan not only makes your patio and walkways more useful at night, it gives these spaces a second life with a completely different feel from the daytime setting.

Standard low-voltage lighting systems are commonly available in complete kits that include a low-voltage transformer, low-voltage cable, and several light fixtures, each with a wire lead that links to the main cable with a special connector. A basic landscape kit typically has three or more fixtures for standard in-ground installation. If you'd like to add specialty patio fixtures, such as step (or "brick") lights, pole- and wall-mount fixtures, and task lights for outdoor cooking, make sure your system is compatible with a full range of accessory lights. In addition to standard wired systems, you can find a wide variety of solar-powered fixtures that offer free operation and the easiest possible installation.

Here are some other factors to consider when choosing a standard low-voltage lighting system:

- **Transformer power**—For best performance, the total wattage of the light fixtures should be at least one-third of the transformer's wattage rating but should not exceed the wattage rating. If necessary, use two systems to avoid overloading a single system with too many fixtures.
- **Transformer controls**—Consider timers and photosensitive switches for automatic operation.
- **Cable gauge size**—12-amp UF cable is recommended to reduce voltage drop, resulting in dimmer lights at the far end of the line. Long cable runs may require 8- or 10-gauge wire to prevent voltage drop.
- **Fixture and bulb brightness**—Brightness is often rated in foot-candles: one foot-candle is equivalent to the brightness of a 12" square area lighted by a candle held 12" away. Use the brightness rating to guide the fixture layout.

As with indoor light fixtures, landscape lights can be just as beautiful as they are illuminating. Consider the look (and visibility) of fixtures in the daylight, in addition to their lighting characteristics at night.

Tools & Materials ▸

Drill and bits	Paint stir-stick
Screwdrivers	PVC pipe
Trenching spade	Hammer
Low-voltage lighting kit	Work gloves

Effective Lighting ▶

Here are some general design guidelines to keep in mind when planning your lighting scheme:

Keep it subtle. With the exception of surprise-oriented security lights (floodlights, motion detectors), outdoor lighting should be mellow and subdued—an intermingling of soft light and shadows, not a battle against the darkness.

Mix it up. The best lighting plans employ a combination of fixtures and levels of illumination. Use brighter or more direct lights to highlight a few landscape features or patio areas. Otherwise, stick to low, unobtrusive lighting. Variation helps emphasize key elements.

Illuminate surfaces, not people. Orient fixtures downward to light up paths and patio surfaces or upward for indirect background lighting. As a general rule, naked bulbs should be hidden from view. Never direct beams of light into a viewer's line of sight, which creates a harsh glare at night.

Use the right fixture for the job. There's an outdoor light for virtually every application. Some are decorative and made to be visible; others are easy to hide under low plantings or tuck away in the shadows.

Illuminate appropriately: Patios call for atmospheric lighting for nighttime use—so party guests can see one another (at least in dim light) and diners can see their food during evening meals. Provide a soft wash of background light with sconces mounted to the house wall or with post-fixtures with globes. For entertaining, a sprinkling of small accent lights along the patio's borders can create enough light for socializing while maintaining subtle ambiance.

Consider safety: Main traffic routes on and off a patio need lighting for safe and convenient travel. On patios, include lights at all changes in floor height and on any obstructions not clearly visible at night. Recessed lights on step risers provide a small amount of light precisely where it's needed. Paths are best lighted with low-voltage pole fixtures; space fixtures 8 to 10 ft. apart for localized pools of light, or put them closer together to overlap their washes of light in a "spread" pattern.

Typical low-voltage outdoor lighting systems consist of: lens cap (A), lens cap posts (B), upper reflector (C), lens (D), base/stake/cable connector assembly (contains lower reflector) (E), low-voltage cable (F), lens hood (G), 7-watt 12-volt bulbs (H), cable connector caps (I), control box containing transformer and timer (J), and light sensor (K).

How to Install Low-Voltage Patio Lighting

Determine where you will install the transformer(s)— either in the garage, on an exterior house wall, or on an outdoor post buried in the ground with concrete. If installing the transformer in the garage, mount it on a wall within 24" of a GFCI receptacle and at least 12" above the floor. See variation (below) for alternative installations.

Drill a hole through the wall or rim joist for the low-voltage cable and any sensors to pass through (inset). If a circuit begins in a high-traffic area, it's a good idea to protect the cable by running it through a short piece of PVC pipe or conduit and then into the shallow trench (see step 9).

Planning Tip ▸

Make a diagram of your yard and mark the location of new fixtures. Note the wattages of the fixtures and use the diagram to select a transformer and plan the circuits.

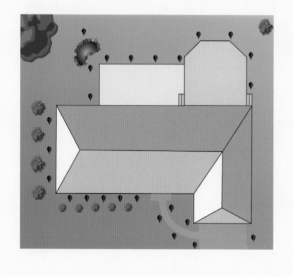

Variation: To install the transformer(s) to an outdoor wall or post, mount the unit within 24" of an outdoor GFCI receptacle and at least 12" above the ground. If the receptacle is exposed, install an "in-use" receptacle cover for added protection from the elements. Do not use an extension cord to connect the transformer.

3

Attach the end of the low-voltage wire to the terminals on the transformer. Make sure that both strands of wire are held tightly by their terminal screws.

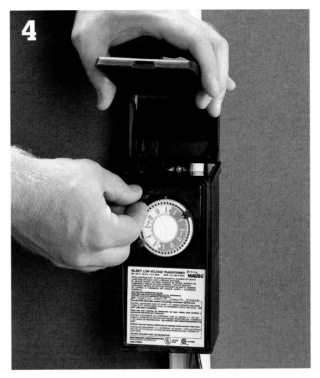

4

Transformers usually have a simple mechanism that allows you to set times for the lights to come on and go off automatically. Set these times before hanging the transformer.

5

Many low-voltage light fixtures are modular, consisting of a spiked base, a riser tube and a lamp. On these units, feed the wires and the wire connector from the light section down through the riser tube and into the base.

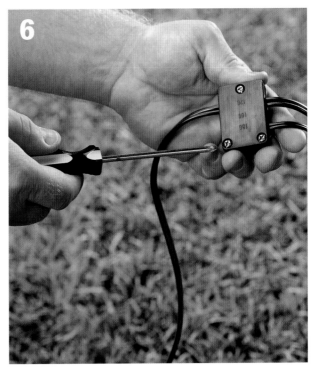

6

Take apart the connector box and insert the ends of the fixture wire and the low voltage landscape cable into it. Puncture the wire ends with the connector box leads. Reassemble the connector box.

(continued)

Feed the wire connector back into the light base and attach it according to directions that came with the lamp. In this model, all that was required was pushing the connector into a locking slot in the base.

After the bulb is installed, assemble the fixture parts that cover it, including the lens cap and reflector.

Lay out the lights, with the wires attached, in the pattern you have chosen. Then cut the sod between fixtures with a spade. Push the blade about 5" deep and pry open a seam by rocking the blade back and forth.

Gently force the cable into the slot formed by the spade; don't tear the wire insulation. A paint stick (or a cedar shingle) is a good tool for this job. Push the wire to the bottom of the slot.

Once the lamp is stabilized, tuck any extra wire into the slot using the paint stick. If you have a lot of extra wire, you can fold it and push the excess to the bottom of the slot. No part of the wire should be exposed when you are done with the job.

Firmly push the light into the slot in the sod. It the lamp doesn't seat properly, pull it out and cut another slot at a right angle to the first and try again.

Choosing Solar Landscape Lights ▶

Outdoor solar-powered lighting offers two distinct advantages over conventional low-voltage systems: easy, flexible installation and free power. Installing most landscape and patio light fixtures is as simple as staking the light into the ground or mounting it to a wall or post. Many fixtures, including path and accent lights, have a built-in solar panel, so the fixture can go anywhere it will be exposed to direct sunlight during the day. Brighter fixtures, like spot and security lights, often include a separate solar panel with a thin wire that delivers power to the light. The panel is mounted and positioned for maximum sun exposure, while the light fixture can be placed directly where it's needed. Most solar fixtures come with a photosensitive switch that automatically turns the light on at dusk and off at sunrise.

The main disadvantage of solar lighting is reliability. Lower quality fixtures and some high-power lights (such as spot lights) offer running times that won't last through the night. To minimize this problem, choose high-quality fixtures with advanced solar cells (better cells collect more power in low-light weather than cheaper cells) and efficient LED bulbs.

Solar landscape lights are available in sets and individual fixtures. You can pick and choose fixtures based on lighting needs as well as the fixtures' appearance and brightness. Best of all, you can easily reposition lights for desired effects throughout the seasons.

Conversion Charts

Metric Equivalent

	1/64	1/32	1/25	1/16	1/8	1/4	3/8	2/5	1/2	5/8	3/4	7/8	1	2	3	4	5	6	7	8	9	10	11	12	36	39.4
Inches (in.)	1/64	1/32	1/25	1/16	1/8	1/4	3/8	2/5	1/2	5/8	3/4	7/8	1	2	3	4	5	6	7	8	9	10	11	12	36	39.4
Feet (ft.)																								1	3	3 1/12
Yards (yd.)																									1	1 1/12
Millimeters (mm)	0.40	0.79	1	1.59	3.18	6.35	9.53	10	12.7	15.9	19.1	22.2	25.4	50.8	76.2	101.6	127	152	178	203	229	254	279	305	914	1,000
Centimeters (cm)							0.95	1	1.27	1.59	1.91	2.22	2.54	5.08	7.62	10.16	12.7	15.2	17.8	20.3	22.9	25.4	27.9	30.5	91.4	100
Meters (m)																								.30	.91	1.00

Converting Measurements

To Convert:	To:	Multiply by:
Inches	Millimeters	25.4
Inches	Centimeters	2.54
Feet	Meters	0.305
Yards	Meters	0.914
Miles	Kilometers	1.609
Square inches	Square centimeters	6.45
Square feet	Square meters	0.093
Square yards	Square meters	0.836
Cubic inches	Cubic centimeters	16.4
Cubic feet	Cubic meters	0.0283
Cubic yards	Cubic meters	0.765
Pints (U.S.)	Liters	0.473 (Imp. 0.568)
Quarts (U.S.)	Liters	0.946 (Imp. 1.136)
Gallons (U.S.)	Liters	3.785 (Imp. 4.546)
Ounces	Grams	28.4
Pounds	Kilograms	0.454
Tons	Metric tons	0.907

To Convert:	To:	Multiply by:
Millimeters	Inches	0.039
Centimeters	Inches	0.394
Meters	Feet	3.28
Meters	Yards	1.09
Kilometers	Miles	0.621
Square centimeters	Square inches	0.155
Square meters	Square feet	10.8
Square meters	Square yards	1.2
Cubic centimeters	Cubic inches	0.061
Cubic meters	Cubic feet	35.3
Cubic meters	Cubic yards	1.31
Liters	Pints (U.S.)	2.114 (Imp. 1.76)
Liters	Quarts (U.S.)	1.057 (Imp. 0.88)
Liters	Gallons (U.S.)	0.264 (Imp. 0.22)
Grams	Ounces	0.035
Kilograms	Pounds	2.2
Metric tons	Tons	1.1

Converting Temperatures

Convert degrees Fahrenheit (F) to degrees Celsius (C) by following this simple formula: Subtract 32 from the Fahrenheit temperature reading. Then mulitply that number by $5/9$. For example, 77°F - 32 = 45. 45 $\times$ $5/9$ = 25°C.

To convert degrees Celsius to degrees Fahrenheit, multiply the Celsius temperature reading by $9/5$, then add 32. For example, 25°C $\times$ $9/5$ = 45. 45 + 32 = 77°F.

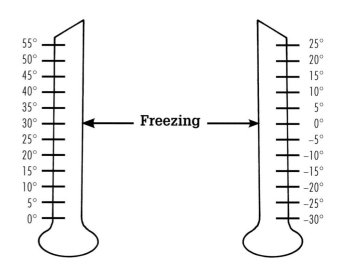

Fahrenheit　　　**Celsius**

Freezing

Drill Bit Guide

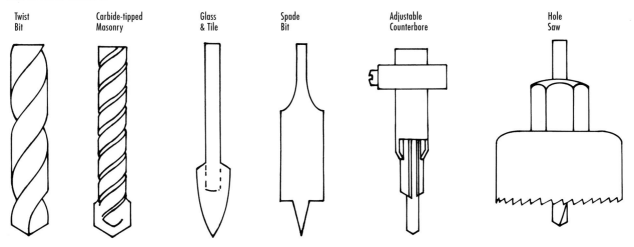

Twist Bit	Carbide-tipped Masonry	Glass & Tile	Spade Bit	Adjustable Counterbore	Hole Saw

Nails

Nail lengths are identified by numbers from 4 to 60 followed by the letter "d," which stands for "penny." For general framing and repair work, use common or box nails. Common nails are best suited to framing work where strength is important. Box nails are smaller in diameter than common nails, which makes them easier to drive and less likely to split wood. Use box nails for light work and thin materials. Most common and box nails have a cement or vinyl coating that improves their holding power.

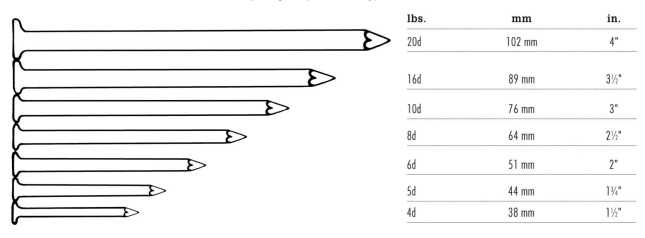

lbs.	mm	in.
20d	102 mm	4"
16d	89 mm	3½"
10d	76 mm	3"
8d	64 mm	2½"
6d	51 mm	2"
5d	44 mm	1¾"
4d	38 mm	1½"

Counterbore, Shank & Pilot Hole Diameters

Screw Size	Counterbore Diameter for Screw Head (in inches)	Clearance Hole for Screw Shank (in inches)	Pilot Hole Diameter	
			Hard Wood (in inches)	Soft Wood (in inches)
#1	9/64	5/64	3/64	1/32
#2	1/4	3/32	3/64	1/32
#3	1/4	7/64	1/16	3/64
#4	1/4	1/8	1/16	3/64
#5	1/4	1/8	5/64	1/16
#6	5/16	9/64	3/32	5/64
#7	5/16	5/32	3/32	5/64
#8	3/8	11/64	1/8	3/32
#9	3/8	11/64	1/8	3/32
#10	3/8	3/16	1/8	7/64
#11	1/2	3/16	5/32	9/64
#12	1/2	7/32	9/64	1/8

Resources

Belgard
p. 11 Pavers and retaining walls
877 235 4273
www.belgard.biz

Borgert Products, Inc.
p. 63 (top) Concrete pavers and walls
800 622 4952
www.borgertproducts.com

Crossville Porcelain Tile
p. 19
931 484 2110
www.crossvilleinc.com

Ezydeck™
p. 120 (product also shown on page 121) modular decking
  system
800 343 6394
www.ezydeck.com / www.floorings.com

Municipal Code Corporation
Online library database available to public of city/county
  ordinances
www.municode.com

North American One-Call Referral System
888 258 0808

Underdeck
p. 196 Inter-joist ceiling system
877 805 7156
www.underdeck.com

ScreenTight
p. 228 Porch screening
800 768 7325
www.screentight.com

Palram Americas
p. 206 Sunturf corrugated polycarbonate building panels and
  Palsun flat extruded polycarbonate sheeting
800 999 9459
www.palramamericas.com

Red Wing Shoes Co.
work shoes and boots shown throughout book
800 733 9464
www.redwingshoes.com

Photography Credits

Belgard / www.belgard.biz
p. 11

Borgert
p. 63 (top)

Crossville Porcelain Tile
p. 19

Distinctive Designs
p. 197 (lower)

Ezydeck™ modular decking system / www.ezydeck.com /
  www.floorings.com
p. 3 (right column, second from top), 120 (product also
  shown on page 121)

John Deere
p. 164 (lower)

Tony Giammarino / www.tonygiammarino.com
p. 38–39, 63 (lower right), 75 (lower), 80

iStock Photography / www.istockphoto.com
p. 88 (two lower images), 172, 188 (lower two), 198 (lower
  left and right), 249

Shelley Metcalf
p. 4, 6–7, 9 (lower), 10, 15, 25, 38, 114, 194–195 (114 and
195 William Bocken Architecture & Interior Design, Paul
Adams Landscape Design

Jerry Pavia
p. 17, 18 (right), 74, 130 (top), 138–139, 140 (two lower), 166,
  175 (lower two), 186, 188 (top two)

Photolibrary / Garden Picture Library /
  www.photolibrary.com
p. 8 © Clive Nichols, 9 (top) © Ed Badham, 12 © Allan Pollok-
  Morris, 16 © Ron Sutherland, 21 (top) Photolibrary/GPL, 24
  © Jennifer Cheung/Botanica/GPL, 140 (top) © Allan Pollok-
  Morris, 163 Garden Picture Library, 192 Photolibrary

Versa-LOK® Retaining Wall Systems /
  www.versa-lok.com
p. 13, 22

Jessie Walker
p. 14

Index

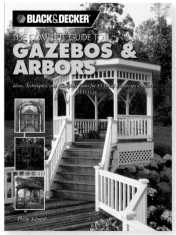
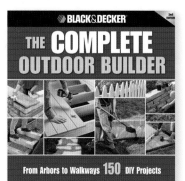
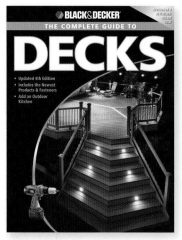